The **RESTART** Cookbook

*Delicious, no-sugar-added recipes
for your real food lifestyle.*

ISBN: 978-0-9968894-0-7

2nd Edition revised and edited by Heather Fischer-Page.

Collaborators

Jeni Hall, NTP
The RESTART® Program
www.therestartprogram.com
info@therestartprogram.com

Lisa Havens, NTP, RWP
Real Vibrance
www.realvibrance.com
lisa.realvibrance@gmail.com

Kariman Pierce, NTP, CGP
New Gratitude Nutrition
www.newgratitudenutrition.com
newgratitudetucson@gmail.com

Tiana Rockwell, NTP
Tri Real Food
www.TriRealFood.com
info@trirealfood.com

Jennifer Steakley, NTP, LMT
Wellness Nutrition & Bodywork
thatwellnessplace.com
jen@thatwellnessplace.com

Mary Budinger, NTC
Mary's Apple Nutrition
www.MarysApple.com
budinger@earthlink.net

Jennifer Konow LMT, NTP
Pure Palate
www.MyPurePalate.com
Jennifer@MyPurePalate.com

Caroline Fogg, NTC
Optimal Health Nutritional Therapy
www.optimalhealth-nutritionaltherapy.com
ohnutritionaltherapy@gmail.com

Jessica Bischof, NTC
Simple Steps Nutrition
www.SimpleStepsNutrition.com
jessica@simplestepsnutrition.com

Aypril Porter, NTP, RWP
Living Matters Nutrition
www.livingmattersnutrition.com
info@livingmattersnutrition.com

Courtney Cronk, MA, NTP
Nourish Portland
www.nourishportland.com
courtney@nourishportland.com

Hollis Baley, NTP
Nutrition By Hollis
www.NutritionByHollis.com
NutritionByHollis@gmail.com

Annette Steward, NTP
My Renewed Vitality
www.myrenewedvitality.com
myrenewedvitality@gmail.com

Angela R. Lewis, NTC
Temple Fuel Nutritional Therapy
www.templefuelnutrition.com
templefuel@msn.com

Tara Chatterton, NTP, QHHT, ECP
Radiant You - Holistic Solutions
www.radiantyoupdx.com
heal@radiantyoupdx.com

Jessica Kouka, NTP
Arise Nutritional Therapy
www.arisenutritionaltherapy.com
arisenutritionaltherapy@comcast.net

Tricia Class, NTC
Class Nutritional Therapy
www.classnt.com
tricia.class@gmail.com

Nancy Sullivan, NTP
Cape Ann Nutritional Therapy
canutritionaltherapy@gmail.com

Linda Tompkins, NTC
Fresh Simple Balance
www.freshsimplebalance.com
linda@freshsimplebalance.com

Heather Fischer-Page, NTP
Healthy Decadence
www.healthydecadencentp.com
healthydecadencentp@gmail.com

Bev Alam, NTC
Nutrition With Bev
www.nutritionwithbev.com
bevalam@gmail.com

Chelo Gable, NTP
Vashon Nutritional Therapy
csgable559@gmail.com

Sarah Barsotti, NTP, LMT, HHC
Bountiful Health and Wellness
sarah@bountifulhealthandwellness.com

RESTART®

Contents

Introduction by Jeni Hall, NTP, Creator of The RESTART® Program

What is The RESTART® Program? It is part nutritional class, part sugar detox, and part support group - a powerful and empowering set up for success.

The recipes and suggestions in this book come from a wonderful collaboration of many RESTART® instructors. They share their passion for health and wellness with the RESTART® groups that they teach.

A home-cooked meal is a gift. Every time you prepare nutritious food for someone, even if that someone is just yourself, you are showing them how much you care about them.

Healthy meals never have to be complicated to be delicious. Use these recipes exactly as written, or allow them to be a jumping-off point to inspire your creativity in the kitchen.

Of course, modify or omit any ingredient that you have a known sensitivity or allergy to. You are the master of your own body, always.

We're bringing back the art of cooking real food for real health!

Special thanks to Karley Cunningham of Big Bold Brand! Also deep gratitude to Heather Fischer-Page, Lisa Havens, Sara Lingenfelther, Kariman Pierce, and all of the wonderful RESTART® Instructors who contributed their delicious recipes to this book. We hope you enjoy them!

Jeni

Jeni Hall, NTP
Creator of The RESTART® Program

the **RESTART**® rule:
*"Whatever I eat, I **choose** it consciously, I **enjoy** it thoroughly, and then I **let it go**."*

RESTART®

6

A Note About Sugar

The American Heart Association recommends no more than 6-9 added teaspoons (24-36 grams) of sugar per adult per day and no more than 3 added teaspoons (12 grams) of sugar per child per day. According to Forbes.com, the average American adult is consuming 22 added teaspoons (88 grams) of sugar per person per day. Children are consuming a staggering 32 added teaspoons (128 grams) of sugar per person per day.

The RESTART® Program challenges its participants to consume ZERO grams of added sugar as an important way to "restart" the body. Added sugar is defined as sugar not naturally occurring in food but added to food in the form of high fructose corn syrup, white refined sugar, artificial sweeteners, honey, maple syrup, etc.

The recipes in this resource have NO added sugars. You will be delighted and amazed at how delicious these recipes are!

the 5 and 5 rule:
When choosing foods with labels, look for 5 ingredients or less (that you recognize as real food!) and 5 grams of sugar or less per serving.

A Note About Quality & Ingredients

When buying ingredients for the recipes in this book, it is important to source the highest quality you can find. Local farmers' markets are a great place to start. Many towns have Community Supported Agriculture (CSA) groups where you can buy weekly shares. Most grocery stores offer organic and sometimes local ingredients as well.

High quality is especially important when purchasing protein and animal fats. Animals who have engaged in natural behaviors, enjoyed sunlight and open spaces and who have been allowed to eat foods they are designed to eat, offer protein and fat that contains essential fatty acids that cannot be found in factory farmed products. We want happy cows, chickens, turkeys and goats (to name a few) to have a good life. These healthy animals in turn, benefit us, and we are grateful for their nourishment.

For guidance on making the best produce choices, visit The Environmental Working Group's website for this year's "Dirty Dozen/Clean Fifteen" lists at www.ewg.org.

Whenever possible look for:

- Local, organic grass-fed and pasture-raised meats
- Local, organic grass-fed butter and other animal fats
- Local, organic, raw, virgin, cold-pressed oils
- Local, organic pasture-raised eggs
- Local, organic vegetables and fruits

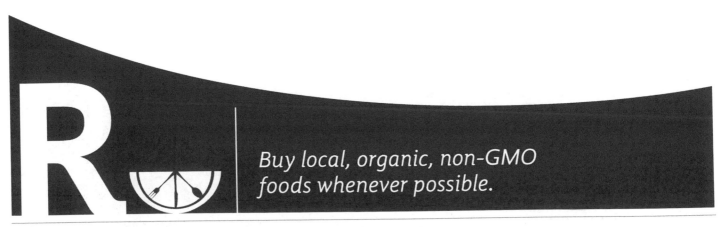

Buy local, organic, non-GMO foods whenever possible.

Recipes

Recipe Key

Labels (marked in bold if included in recipe)
F = Fruits
NS = Nightshade Vegetables
N = Nuts/Seeds

You will see certain ingredients bolded to indicate that they are fruits, nightshades or nuts/seeds. For recipes containing these ingredients, decide if you want to use the recipe as is, remove or replace the ingredient with one your body tolerates, or just skip that recipe.
It's up to you!

Measurements

Tbsp = Tablespoon   **tsp** = Teaspoon   **lb** = Pound

What are NIGHTSHADE Vegetables?

Eggplant   **White potato**   **Paprika**
Tomato   **Tomatillo**
Peppers (green, red, yellow, orange, jalapño, chili, cayenne, pimento)

Nightshades can be a hidden source of inflammation for some people. You may choose to remove them to discover how they affect your body.

Eggs, Frittatas & Omelets

Veggie Frittata

Jeni Hall

Makes 3-4 servings

Ingredients NS

- 2 Tbsp ghee (duck fat is good, too)
- 6 eggs
- ½ onion, sliced thin
- 2 small zucchini, sliced thin
- **½ red bell pepper**
- ¼ c. water
- Salt and pepper to taste

Directions

1. Melt fat in cast iron fry pan or an oven safe pan.
2. Add onion, zucchini and pepper evenly in bottom of pan.
3. Whisk together eggs with water, salt and pepper. Pour egg mixture over the vegetables and cook on low heat until egg begins to set up.
4. Place pan under the broiler on low until golden brown. Remove from oven and let frittata rest for 5-10 minutes.
5. Cut into wedges and serve.

Variations

Add cooked breakfast meats such as chopped ham, bacon or breakfast sausage.

Add some herbs such as basil, oregano and rosemary.

Baked Avocado with Egg

Jeni Hall

Makes 2 servings

Ingredients

- 1 avocado
- 2 eggs
- Salt and pepper to taste

Directions

1. Cut avocado in halves and remove pit. Leave skin on.
2. Separate egg yolk from the whites.
3. Place yolk in center of avocado where pit was located.
4. Sprinkle salt and pepper to taste.
5. Bake at 350 F for 20-25 minutes.

Vegetable Egg Scramble

Heather Page

Makes 2 servings

Ingredients NS

- 2 Tbsp ghee
- 4 eggs
- ¼ **green pepper, diced**
- ¼ red onion, diced
- 5 black or green olives, pitted/sliced
- Handful of spinach
- Salt and pepper to taste

Directions

1. Heat oil in skillet.
2. Sauté onions, pepper until soft.
3. Add eggs and scramble until desired consistency.
4. Add spinach and olives. Sauté another minute or two until heated through.

Variations

Add cooked breakfast meats such as chopped ham, bacon or breakfast sausage.

Add some herbs such as basil, oregano and rosemary.

Baked Eggs with Creamy Spinach
Mary Budinger

Makes 4 servings

Ingredients

- 20 ounces frozen chopped spinach
- 2 Tbsp butter or ghee
- 2 shallots, finely chopped
- 1 cup coconut milk
- ½ tsp sea salt
- 4 eggs

Directions

1. Take the spinach out very first thing in the morning so it can thaw. Place in a strainer. If when you are ready to cook, it is still a bit frozen, run warm water over it until the ice is gone. In either event, press down on the spinach with your hands and a paper towel to remove moisture.

2. Preheat oven to 450 F.

3. In a skillet, melt the butter over medium-low heat. Cook the shallot until soft, 2 minutes.

4. Whisk salt into the coconut milk. Pour into the skillet. Add the spinach. Cook for a minute or so, until the spinach absorbs most of the coconut milk.

5. With a spatula, scrape spinach into an 8×8 pan. Use a spoon to make 4 deep wells that an egg can be dropped into. Crack an egg into each well and bake 7 to 10 minutes, until the whites are set but yokes are still soft. Serve immediately – yum!

Get a head start on your daily intake of nutrient dense leafy greens and good fats by eating a serving first thing in the morning. This recipe is easier than making quiche. It is an easy one-pan meal that tastes really good when made with frozen spinach.

Freezing food preserves the nutrient content, so frozen spinach is often more nutritious than the "fresh" spinach on grocery stores shelves.

~ Mary

Egg Muffins

Jennifer Steakley

Makes 10-12 muffins

Ingredients NS, N

- Dozen (12) pastured eggs
- Add-ins of your choice - (Chopped ham chunks, bacon, mushrooms, spinach, kale, green, yellow or red onions, **bell peppers**, olives, etc.)
- ¼ cup water or **almond** milk (optional)
- Salt and pepper

Directions

1. Preheat oven to 350 F. Line muffin tins with parchment liners.
2. Fill lined tins about half way with add-ins.
3. Whisk eggs with water or almond milk.
4. Add salt and pepper to whisked eggs and pour into tins filling almost to the top.
5. Bake for 25-30 minutes until eggs are set. Remove from oven and cool completely. Store in a freezer safe container. Freeze or refrigerate. Reheat in microwave or toaster to eat.

EASY Breakfast (Egg-Avocado-Sausage-Yum!)

Linda Tompkins

Makes 1-2 servings

Ingredients

- 2 breakfast sausages (check ingredient label for quality/no added sugar)
- ½ small avocado
- 2 pastured eggs
- Cilantro and chives for garnish (optional)

Directions

1. Preheat oven to 375 F. Line muffin pan with 2 liners each.
2. Cook breakfast sausage, then thinly slice and put on bottom of each muffin liner.
3. Cut half an avocado into 4 slices; put 2 in each muffin cup.
4. Crack an egg on top of each muffin cup.
5. Bake for 15-18 minutes (depending how runny or not you like it).
6. Garnish with optional chives and cilantro.

Paradise Eggs Benedict

Lisa Havens

Makes 2 servings

Ingredients NS

- 2 pastured eggs, poached
- 2 slices uncured bacon, cooked
- 2 handfuls spinach
- 1 Tbsp olive oil
- 6 slices avocado
- **1 tomato, sliced**
- 1 recipe Hollandaise Sauce (p. 91)
- Salt and pepper, to taste

Directions

1. Heat olive oil in sauté pan on medium.
2. Add spinach and a pinch of salt to pan and sauté for two minutes.
3. Plate spinach and layer tomato, bacon, avocado, and poached egg.
4. Top with hollandaise sauce.
5. Serve immediately.

Meat

Lamb in Coconut Curry Sauce

Jeni Hall

Makes 4 servings

Ingredients NS

- 2 Tbsp coconut oil
- 1 lb cubed lamb or lamb stew meat
- 1 large onion, chopped
- 3-4 carrots, chopped
- 1 Tbsp grated ginger root
- 3 cloves of garlic
- **2 tsp curry powder**
- 1 tsp sea salt
- ½ cup broth
- 1 cup coconut milk

Directions

1. Melt the coconut oil in a large pot and brown the lamb meat in it. Remove the meat and set aside. Leave fat in bottom of pan.
2. Saute the onions on medium heat until soft (about 10 minutes). Add garlic, ginger and curry powder and continue to saute for a few more minutes. Add carrots and stir to coat them with the spice mixture.
3. Pour in the broth and scrape meat bits off of pan bottom. Pour in coconut milk and bring to simmer.
4. Add the meat back to pan and simmer for 30 minutes.

Kheema Kheema

Tricia Class

Makes 6 servings

Ingredients NS

- 2 Tbsp ghee (or coconut oil)
- 1 ½ cup onions, finely chopped
- 4 cloves garlic, minced
- 1 ½ lbs ground lamb
- ½ tsp ground ginger
- 1 tsp turmeric
- 1 tsp cumin
- 1 cinnamon stick (size does not really matter, just use what you have)

- ¼ tsp cloves
- **½ tsp cayenne (optional or to taste)**
- ½ tsp salt
- **1 cup tomato sauce or tomato puree**
- ½ to 1 cup water
- Cilantro, to taste, as garnish

Directions

1. Heat oil in a heavy bottom pan over medium heat.
2. Add onions and sauté until clear, about 5 minutes.
3. Add garlic. Continue sautéing about 90 seconds.
4. Add ground lamb. On medium heat, continue cooking and breaking up the lamb, about 3 minutes.
5. Add spices, ginger through salt. Sauté about one minute.
6. Add tomato sauce or puree. Continue cooking until it forms a shiny mixture, about 2 minutes.
7. Add water to desired consistency. Bring to a near boil and then turn heat to low. Cover. Simmer covered for 30 minutes.
8. Garnish with fresh chopped cilantro. Use it, but not so much that it overwhelms the dish.

I love all things Persian (Iranian), especially the food. Kheema is similar to Texan Chili (i.e. no beans.) Texan Chili is made with ground or cubed beef and Mexican spices. In India and Persia, Kheema is a similar dish made from ground lamb with Indian or Persian spices. You can use this recipe with mutton or beef as well.

~ Tricia

The **RESTART** Cookbook

Salsa Meatloaf

Tricia Class

Makes 6-8 servings

Ingredients NS, N

- 1 and ½ lbs ground beef
- **1 cup salsa**
- 1 egg, beaten
- 2 garlic cloves, minced or pressed
- **1-2 Tbsp chili powder**
- 2 tsp dried oregano
- 1 tsp ground cumin
- 1 tsp salt
- **¾ cup almond meal**

Directions

1. Preheat oven to 350 F.
2. In a large mixing bowl, mix together all ingredients. Hands work best.
3. Place meat mixture into a 8 x 4 in. loaf pan.
4. Bake for 45 minutes or until internal temperature reaches 170 F.

Taco Salad

Jennifer Steakley

Makes 4 servings

Ingredients NS

- 1 lb. ground beef, ground turkey or ground chicken
- **3-4 Tbsp Homemade Taco Seasoning** (p. 96)
- Salad greens
- **Tomatoes**
- 2 avocados
- ½ purple onion
- ½ can full fat coconut milk
- 1 Tbsp raw apple cider vinegar
- ⅛ tsp pepper
- ½ tsp sea salt
- **Fresh salsa or pico de gallo** (p. 95)

Directions

1. Make taco meat: Brown ground beef, ground turkey or ground chicken. Season with your home made taco seasoning mix and stir well.
2. Make Creamy Avocado Dressing (p. 84)
3. Place taco meat on a bed of salad greens. Add fresh tomatoes, chopped avocado and sliced purple onion. Top with creamy avocado dressing. Can also be topped with just a little plain olive oil instead.

Ground Beef with Cabbage & Kale

Makes 4 servings

Ingredients

- 1 lb. organic ground beef, grass fed
- ½ head cabbage, chopped
- 1 sweet onion, chopped
- 4 stalks kale, washed and torn into 2-3 inch pieces
- Salt and pepper to taste.

Variations

- Add broccoli with cabbage and onions.
- Serve with mashed cauliflower.
- Serve with avocado.
- Add herbs and spices such as thyme, rosemary, oregano, garlic, or **cayenne (NS)**.

Directions

1. Cook beef in large pan until it has just lost the pink. Transfer to separate dish.
2. Add cabbage and onions to pan with beef fat. Cook until tender.
3. Transfer beef back to original pan and add kale.
4. Season with desired spices. Mix and cook until kale is slightly cooked.

Beef Jerky

Caroline Fogg

Makes 4 servings

Ingredients NS

- 1 lb grass-fed ground beef
- Sea salt
- Herbs and spices (optional - oregano, rosemary, thyme, sage, **chili powder**, **paprika**, garlic powder, onion powder, coconut aminos)

Directions:

1. Mix salt and herbs well with ground beef.
2. Place on parchment paper and spread out thinly using heel of hand.
3. Score lines of desired size of jerky using sharp knife.
4. Bake in oven on baking tray at 150F for 10 hours or 145F for 3-4 hours in a dehydrator.
5. Remove jerky and place on plate with paper towel to cool.
6. Break up into slices/pieces and store in refrigerator.

Fajita Steak Wraps
Heather Page

Makes 4 servings

Ingredients NS

- 1 lb. grassfed skirt or flank steak, cut into 4" sections
- 1 small red onion, peeled and diced
- **½ yellow or orange bell pepper, diced**
- **½ green bell pepper, diced**
- 3 Tbsp olive oil
- Romaine or butter lettuce leaves, divided
- Avocado, sliced
- **Pico de Gallo** (p. 95)
- **1 recipe Cauliflower Fried Rice** (p. 58)

Marinade:

- 2 cloves garlic, minced
- **1 jalapeno, seeded and minced**
- ¼ cup cilantro, chopped
- Juice of 1 lime
- ¼ cup olive oil
- ½ tsp cumin
- ¼ tsp salt
- **⅛ tsp cayenne pepper (optional)**

Directions

1. Mix garlic, jalapeno, cilantro, lime juice, oil and spices in a glass bowl. Add steak and marinate for two hours up to overnight. If chilled, let set at room temperature for 30 minutes before grillling.

2. Heat grill pan at medium. Remove steak from marinade add to grill pan. Discard marinade. Cook each side for 2-3 minutes for medium rare, or longer for desired internal temperature.

3. Let rest for 10 minutes before slicing against the grain.

4. While meat is resting, heat olive oil in pan over medium low to medium heat and sauté onion and peppers with salt and pepper until onions are translucent.

5. Place lettuce cups on plate and add steak and vegetables. Top with your choice of avocado and pico de gallo. Serve with a side of cauliflower rice.

 **RESTART®**

 26

Slow Cooker Pot Roast

Heather Page

Makes 6 servings

Ingredients

- 3 lb. grassfed chuck roast
- 2 carrots, peeled and sliced into 3" pieces
- 2 parsnips, peeled and sliced into 3" pieces
- 2 celery stalks, sliced into 3" pieces
- 3 garlic cloves, peeled and whole
- 1 medium yellow onion, peeled and chopped into 2" pieces
- 2 bay leaves
- 1 cup beef broth
- ½ tsp mineral salt
- ½ tsp black pepper

Directions

1. Pour broth into 5-6 quart slow cooker and add vegetables.
2. Lightly season roast and add to slow cooker. Cook on low for 6-8 hours until meat is tender and desired internal temperature.
3. Remove roast and set on serving platter to slice. Place cooked vegetables on side to serve.
4. Remove bay leaves and strain reserved liquid for au jus.
5. (Optional) Serve with Mashed Cauliflower (p. 63).

Basic Meatballs

Kariman Pierce

Makes 18-24 meatballs

Ingredients NS

- 1-2 lbs ground beef
- 1 tsp sea salt
- 1 tsp garlic powder
- ½-1 tsp favorite savory dried herb such as basil, oregano, rosemary

Optional mix-ins

- Finely chopped and sautéed onion
- 1-2 cloves of finely chopped and sautéed garlic
- **1 small can of tomato paste**
- 1 egg

Directions

1. Preheat oven to 350 F.
2. Place ground beef in large bowl and add chosen ingredients.
3. Wash your hands and then blend all ingredients with you bare hands until thoroughly mixed.
4. Form 1-2 inch balls with your hands.
5. Place on a parchment-lined cookie sheet to bake.
6. Bake for 25 minutes or until cooked through.

Cover the cookie sheet with a piece of parchment paper for easier clean up.

~ Kariman

 **RESTART**®

Shredded Pork

Mary Budinger

Makes 6-8 servings

Ingredients NS

- ~3 pounds pork butt or fatty pork meat, including organ meats such as heart
- 1 cup vinegar
- ½ cup lard or ghee or palm oil
- **4 Tbsp chili powder**
- 2 tsp dried oregano
- 4 cloves garlic, minced
- **½ cup tomato paste**
- 2 cups beef or chicken broth

Directions

1. Cut pork into 1-inch cubes and marinate in vinegar about 24 hours, refrigerated.
2. Dry cubes well and brown in fat in a large casserole with lid.
3. Add remaining ingredients and bring to a boil.
4. Reduce to a simmer and place in a 350 F oven, with the lid slightly askew so moisture can evaporate.
5. Bake several hours until the liquid is reduced to about half.
6. Shred the pork with a fork or knife.
7. Makes about 4 cups.

Variations

This recipe can be done in the slow cooker. Use directions above to marinate and brown, then add pork and rest of ingredients to slow cooker. Cook on low for 6 hours or until meat is tender and at preferred internal temperature. Shred and serve as listed above.

Sautéed Pancetta, Fennel & Celery

Sarah Barsotti

Makes 4 servings

Ingredients

- 4 oz diced pancetta
- 2 fennel bulbs sliced
- 2 small celery bunches sliced
- Salt and pepper to taste

Directions

1. In a large sauté pan, sauté pancetta over medium high heat.
2. Toss in sliced fennel and celery.
3. Season with a little salt and fresh ground pepper.

Pork, Fennel & Apple Meatballs

Tricia Class

Makes 18-24 meatballs

Ingredients F

- 1 and ½ lbs ground pork
- 1 tsp ground fennel seeds
- **1 green apple, grated**
- 1 egg
- 1 Tbsp coconut flour (optional)
- ½ tsp sea salt
- ½ tsp black pepper

Directions

1. Combine all ingredients in a large bowl.
2. Mix thoroughly with hands.
3. Scoop by tablespoon onto a parchment-lined baking sheet.
4. Bake for 10-15 minutes at 350 F or until cooked through.

Breakfast Hash

Heather Page

Makes 4 servings

Ingredients

- 1 lb of breakfast pan sausage
- ¼ cup onions, diced
- ½ cup parsnips, peeeled and chopped
- ¼ cup red and/or golden beets, peeled and chopped
- 8-10 Brussels sprouts, quartered
- 1 cup kale, chopped
- 3 Tbsp coconut oil
- Salt and pepper to taste

Directions

1. Melt coconut oil in skillet over medium heat.
2. Add sausage and vegetables to skillet. Sauté for a few minutes until sausage is lightly browned, then cover.
3. Stir every couple of minutes so sausage doesn't burn. Cook until sausage is done and vegetables are firm, but tender.
4. Add kale at end and cook for 3-5 minutes until kale is tender. Salt and pepper to taste.

Tip

This is a great dish to prep on Sunday and have for the week. On a busy weekday morning, simply reheat a single serving of hash. Cook 1-2 eggs in butter, ghee or coconut oil and serve with hash. You now have breakfast in less than 5 minutes!

Poultry

Ann's Turkey Meatballs

Tricia Class

Makes 12 meatballs

Sauce Ingredients NS

- 1 Tbsp olive oil
- 1 medium onion, chopped
- 4 cloves garlic, minced
- **3 Tbsp tomato paste**
- **1 (28-ounce) can crushed tomatoes, liquid included**
- **1 can green chilies**
- 2 tsp chopped oregano leaves
- 1 sprig fresh rosemary
- Sea salt
- ¼ cup torn fresh basil leaves

Meatballs Ingredients N

- 1 lb ground turkey meat, NOT super lean
- **¼ cup almond meal**
- ½ cup finely grated carrot
- ½ cup finely chopped onion
- 2 large cloves garlic, minced
- 2 Tbsp minced fresh parsley leaves, plus more for garnish
- 2 tsp minced fresh thyme leaves
- 1 egg, lightly beaten
- ½ tsp sea salt

(recipe continued)

Make Sauce:

1. In a 4-quart saucepan, heat the oil over medium heat.
2. Sauté the onions until translucent, about 3 minutes, then add the garlic and cook for 1 minute more.
3. Add tomato paste, tomatoes, chilies, oregano, rosemary, and salt. Bring all the ingredients to a low boil, reduce heat and cook for approximately 15 minutes, until liquid has evaporated slightly.
4. Season with salt and pepper, to taste.
5. While sauce is cooking, make meatballs.

Prepare Meatballs:

1. Preheat the broiler and grease a baking sheet with butter, olive oil, or coconut oil.
2. Combine the turkey with all other ingredients in a large work bowl.
3. Form into 2 ½ inch balls and place on a baking sheet.
4. Broil for 10 minutes, or until browned and almost cooked through. (The meatballs will continue to cook once placed in the sauce).
5. Meanwhile, remove rosemary sprig from sauce and add fresh basil. Add the meatballs to the sauce, cover, and cook additional 10 minutes, or until sauce has slightly thickened and meatballs have absorbed some of the sauce.

I received this recipe from my girlfriend, Ann. She and her five sisters were taking part in a 'Meals Across the Miles' project as a way to stay in touch while they were spread out across the country. One of the sisters would pick out a recipe, and then everyone would make it on a certain date. Then they compared notes. I thought this idea was such a cool way to connect with family that I proposed doing this with my sister, cousin, and two aunts. We kept it going for about a year and then life just got a bit crazy (grad school, pregnancy, etc.). But I cherished the experience. And I am so thankful to Ann for sharing this recipe with us.

~ Tricia

Curried Chicken Burgers

Tricia Class

Makes 6 servings

Ingredients NS, F

- 1 and ½ lbs. ground chicken
- **1 green apple, shredded**
- 1 medium onion, shredded
- **1-2 Tbsp sweet curry powder** (adjust to taste)
- ½ tsp sea salt
- ½ tsp black pepper
- Cilantro, to taste
- 1-2 Tbsp olive oil or coconut oil

Directions

1. Mix all ingredients in a bowl.
2. Shape into 6 equal size patties.
3. Heat olive or coconut oil in a medium skillet over high heat. Add three of the burgers at a time.

These burgers are super easy to make and keep well in the fridge for a day or two. Think leftovers for breakfast and lunch. They are high in protein and packed with flavor.

~ Tricia

Spicy Slow Cooker Chicken

Mary Budinger

Makes 2-4 servings

Ingredients NS

- 4-6 organic boneless chicken thighs
- **1 14.5oz can organic diced tomatoes**
- **1 red bell pepper, julienned**
- 1 large yellow onion, julienned
- 4 cloves garlic, minced
- 2 Tbsp sugar-free spice rub (recipe follows)
- fresh limes, **salsa**, guacamole and/or cilantro

Spice Rub Ingredients

- 4 Tbsp unrefined sea salt
- **4 Tbsp smoked paprika**
- 2 Tbsp black pepper
- 2 Tbsp garlic powder
- 2 tsp onion powder
- 1 tsp ground celery seeds (optional, for garnish)
- 1 tsp dried oregano
- **1 tsp chipotle powder**

Directions

1. Place the chicken thighs on the bottom of a slow cooker.
2. Sprinkle 2 Tbsp spice rub over the chicken thighs (save the remaining spice rub for future recipes).
3. Pour the entire can of tomatoes on top of the chicken. Top with onions, garlic and peppers.
4. Cook on high for 3-4 hours or on low for 6-8 hours.
5. Remove chicken thighs and shred with 2 forks. Top with remaining sauce from the slow cooker. Garnish with lime wedges (optional).

Can be served with vegetable noodles, spaghetti squash or in a lettuce cup. Top with fresh salsa, fresh cilantro or guacamole.

~ Mary

Indian Cauliflower Curry with Asparagus & Chicken

Heather Page

Makes 4 servings

Ingredients NS

- 2 Tbsp coconut oil
- ½ medium yellow onion, dked
- **½ red bell pepper, diced**
- 1 head cauliflower, washed and cut into small florets.
- 12 stalks asparagus, cut into 1-inch pieces
- 2 cups cooked chicken, shredded
- ¾ tsp cinnamon
- ¾ tsp ginger
- ¾ tsp turmeric
- ½ tsp cumin
- ½ tsp salt
- ¼ tsp pepper
- ¾ cup chicken bone broth
- 1 cup full fat coconut milk
- fresh cilantro to garnish (optional)

Directions

1. Heat coconut oil in large pan over medium heat.
2. Add onion, red pepper, cauliflower and asparagus in pan and sauté for 5 minutes.
3. Add chicken and sauté another 2 minutes.
4. Add turmeric, cumin, salt, pepper, cinnamon, and ginger and stir to blend spices well.
5. Add broth and coconut milk, and bring to a boil. Reduce heat to simmer covered for about 5 minutes.

Variations

For a little spice, add up to a **¼ tsp cayenne**.

Coconut Curry with Chicken

Caroline Fogg

Makes 2 servings

Ingredients NS

- 1 Tbsp coconut oil
- 2 cloves garlic, chopped
- 1 medium onion, diced
- ½ Tbsp turmeric
- ½ Tbsp cumin
- 1 Tbsp coriander
- 1 small onion
  (or ½ tsp onion powder)
- 1 can (13.5 oz) full fat coconut milk

- 2 stalks celery, chopped
- 1 cup chopped veggies (can be thinly sized carrots, florets of broccoli, zucchini, **bell peppers**, snap peas, etc)
- 1 cup water
- 1 chicken breast, cooked and cut into bit size pieces
- 1 avocado, sliced

Directions

1. Chop the garlic and set aside.
2. Heat large skillet on medium heat and put in the coconut oil.
3. Chop the onion. About now the oil is hot, so add onion and sauté for 5 minutes.
4. Add turmeric, cumin, coriander. Mix to coat onions.
5. Add celery and vegetables, cooked chicken, and coconut milk.
6. Let simmer 10-15 minutes to mix flavors and soften the vegetables.
7. Stir in the garlic at the very end and serve with sliced avocado on top.

Variations

Serve over riced caulfilower or mashed cauliflower (p. 63).

Add **cashew nuts (N)** when you add the chicken and coconut milk.

Stir-Fry Chicken

Caroline Fogg

Makes 4 servings

Ingredients

- 1 lb organic chicken breast
- 2+ Tbsp coconut oil
- 2-4 cloves garlic, crushed
- ½ inch fresh, chopped ginger
- 1 Tbsp fresh lime juice (optional)
- 1 onion
- 2 carrots
- 1 medium head broccoli

- 1 cup snow peas
- 1 ¼ head of cabbage
- 1 bunch bok choy
- 1-2 Tbsp coconut aminos
- 1 pkg kelp noodles, rinsed
- 2 Tbsp chicken broth
- 1 bunch chopped cilantro
- Sea salt to taste

Directions

1. Wash and pat dry chicken breast.
2. Cut into bite sized pieces and sprinkle sea salt.
3. Wash, dry and cut all vegetables.
4. In large frying pan or wok heat up oil.
6. Add onions and cook till translucent.
7. Add chicken and cook for a minute or two. Add chicken broth.
8. Add all vegetables except bok choy.
9. Add garlic and ginger.
10. Cook, stirring frequently.
11. Add bok choy towards the end.
12. Add 1-2 Tbsp coconut aminos.
13. Add kelp noodles.
13 Squeeze lime juice on top and mix in.
14. Add cilantro and serve.

Roast Chicken

Caroline Fogg

Makes 6 servings

Ingredients

- 1 4-5 lb. whole organic chicken
- Fresh rosemary or tarragon chopped
- Fresh lemon juice (optional)
- Salt

Directions

1. Wash and pat dry chicken.
2. Sprinkle salt and herbs all over.
3. Place on its side in roasting pan in oven 350 F.
4. After 20 minutes take out of oven and switch sides and put back in oven.
5. After 20 minutes take out of oven and place on its back. Squeeze fresh lemon juice all over chicken and inside cavity.
6. Bake until done, another 30 to 40 minutes.

Tip

Don't throw that carcass away! See p. 82 for a recipe for chicken bone broth!

Chicken Wings

Caroline Fogg

Makes 6 servings

Ingredients

- 2 lbs. organic chicken wings
- Celtic sea salt

Directions

1. Wash and pat dry chicken wings.
2. Sprinkle salt on both sides.
3. Place on parchment lined baking tray with skin closest to heat source in oven.
4. Bake in oven 425 F for 20 minutes.

Variations

For buffalo wings, heat 4 tbsp butter or ghee and ⅓ cup **hot sauce (NS)** in pan to make wing sauce. Separate wing sauce in half and set reserve sauce aside. Toss chicken wings in half of the wing sauce and marinate for 30 minutes. Remove wings from marinade and place on parchment lined baking sheet. Discard marinade. Bake as shown above. Serve with remaining wing sauce, celery and Creamy Garlic Dressing (p. 85) or Ranch Dressing (p. 84).

Slow Cooker Chicken Cacciatore

Jessica Bischof

Makes 4-6 servings

Ingredients NS

- 4 chicken breasts, or 6-8 thighs
- **1 jar of organic, no sugar-added marinara**
- **2 bell peppers, sliced**
- 2 large zucchini, julienned or spiralized (optional)

Directions

1. Mix all ingredients in crock pot and cook over low heat 8 hours or high heat 4 hours until chicken is cooked through and tender.
2. Serve over zucchini noodles.

Baked Rosemary Chicken

Caroline Fogg

Makes 4-6 servings

Ingredients

- 2 lbs. bone-in chicken thighs and drumsticks
- Fresh rosemary chopped
- Fresh garlic chopped (optional)
- Fresh lemon (optional)
- Sea Salt

Directions

1. Wash and pat dry chicken pieces.
2. Sprinkle rosemary, salt, pepper on top.
3. Spread garlic under the skin.
4. Squeeze lemon on top.
5. Bake in oven 350 F for 40 minutes.

*Be creative and play with other herbs
and spices for variation!*

~ Caroline

Basic Slow Cooker Chicken

Kariman Pierce

Makes 6 servings

Ingredients

- 1 4-5 lb. whole chicken
- 1 tsp sea salt
- 1 tsp garlic powder
- 1 dash of pepper (optional)

Directions

1. Place chicken and spices in crockpot and turn on low.
2. Cook for 6-8 hours.

Tip

Don't throw that carcass away! See p. 82 for a recipe for chicken bone broth!

Slow cookers are very versatile. Try this same method with other cuts of meat (cooking times may vary). It is such an easy way to have dinner ready when you get home each night!

~ Kariman

Bacon Wrapped Chicken

Kariman Pierce

Makes 4-6 servings

Ingredients

- 2-4 boneless chicken breasts OR 6-8 boneless chicken thighs
- 1 package of bacon
- 1 sprig of rosemary
- 1 tsp sea salt
- Garlic powder to taste (optional)

Directions

1. Cut chicken into 1 inch thick, short strips.
2. Place strips in a bowl and add salt, minced rosemary and garlic. Allow spices to coat chicken.
3. Wrap each chicken strip with a strip of bacon-- securely with small amount of overlap.
4. Place "wraps" on baking sheet lined with parchment paper.
5. Bake at 350 F for 25 minutes or until bacon has crispy edges.

 **RESTART**

Fish & Seafood

Prosciutto-Wrapped Salmon

Tricia Class

Makes 6 servings

Ingredients

- 6 (5-ounces) center-cut pieces of wild-caught salmon fillet, skinned
- 12 very thin slices prosciutto (about ¼ pound)
- 2 Tbsp olive oil

Directions

1. Preheat oven to 400 F.
2. Wrap each piece of salmon in a slice of prosciutto, leaving ends of salmon exposed.
3. Place salmon, seam sides down, on an oiled large baking sheet.
4. Season with salt and pepper and drizzle each piece with ½ tsp oil.
5. Bake in middle of oven until just cooked through, 7 to 8 minutes.

Scallops with Shiitake Mushrooms in Ginger Sauce

Mary Budinger

Makes 4 servings

Ingredients

- 2 Tbsp ghee or coconut oil
- 1 lb large sea scallops
- 3 cloves of minced garlic
- 1 medium onion, finely chopped
- ½ inch piece of ginger root, grated
- 1 ½ tsp salt
- 1 cup sliced shiitake mushrooms
- 1 cup snow peas
- ¼ cup broth or water
- 2-3 green onions

Directions

1. Melt the oil or ghee in a large skillet.
2. Rinse and dry scallops.
3. Brown scallops on both sides (1-2 minutes per side) and remove to a plate and set aside.
4. Add onions to melted fat and cook until soft (add more fat if necessary).
5. Add ginger and salt, stir and saute for several minutes.
6. Add broth or water.
7. Add vegetables and continue to saute until they are cooked (about 5 minutes).
8. Pour vegetable and sauce mixture over scallops and stir.
9. Taste and adjust the seasonings if necessary and sprinkle the top of dish with green onions before serving.

Simple Salmon with Asparagus

Mary Budinger

Makes 2-4 servings

Ingredients

- 2 wild Alaskan salmon fillets (5-8 ounces each)
- Coconut oil
- Fresh asparagus spears
- Ground black pepper

Sauce

- 2 Tbsp coconut or extra virgin olive oil
- 1 ½ Tbsp fresh parsley, chopped
- 1 ½ Tbsp fresh dill, chopped
- 3 Tbsp mustard
- 1 clove garlic, minced
- 1-2 Tbsp lemon juice

Directions

1. Put salmon on large rimmed, parchment-lined baking sheet.
2. Coat both sides with oil and liberally sprinkle with salt and pepper.
3. Place salmon in COLD oven on the bottom rack.
4. Heat oven to 400 F.
5. Cook for about 25 minutes until salmon is heated through and flaky.
6. Meanwhile, place asparagus spears in a pan, drizzle with olive oil and pepper, sauté on medium high heat for 1 ½ minutes (al dente, not squishy soft).
7. Combine sauce ingredients and drizzle over salmon before serving.

Optional: Sprinkle seasoned salmon with minced garlic and sliced shallots before placing in the oven. Add sliced almonds (N) for a crunch 3-5 minutes before salmon is cooked through.

~ Mary

Mahi Mahi Lettuce Wrap Tacos

Heather Page

Makes 6 servings

Ingredients

- 5 wild caught mahi mahi filets (5-6 ounces each)
- 1 Tbsp olive oil
- 1 lime, juiced
- ½ tsp mineral salt
- 2 cups, red and green cabbage, chopped
- 1-2 heads butter or leaf lettuce, cleaned and trimmed
- **Pico de Gallo (NS)** (p. 95)
- **Guacamole (NS)** (p. 89)

Directions

1. Marinate mahi mahi in olive oil, lime juice and salt for 30 minutes.
2. Grill for 3-4 minutes each side or to desired internal temperature.
3. Cut or shred cooked mahi mahi and place inside lettuce wrap. May need 1-2 lettuce leaves for "taco" shell.
4. Add guacamole and a little cabbage.
5. Top with pico de gallo.

Niçoise Salad
Angela Lewis

Makes 4 servings

Ingredients NS

- 2- 8oz tuna steaks, grilled (canned tuna can also work)
- 6 hard-boiled eggs, peeled and quartered
- 2 medium heads Boston lettuce, torn into bite-sized pieces
- **3 small ripe tomatoes, cored and cut into eighths**
- 1 small red onion
- 8 ounces green beans, trimmed, halved and boiled 3-5 minutes until crisp
- 2 Tbsp capers, rinsed or several anchovies (optional)
- ½ cup lemon juice

Vinaigrette Ingredients

- ¾ cup extra-virgin olive oil
- 1 medium shallot, minced
- 1 Tbsp minced fresh thyme leaves
- 2 Tbsp minced fresh basil leaves
- 2 tsp minced fresh oregano leaves
- 1 tsp Dijon mustard
- Salt and pepper to taste

Directions

1. Whisk lemon juice, oil, shallot, thyme, basil, oregano, and mustard in medium bowl. Season as needed with salt and pepper.
2. Toss about ¼ of dressing with salad greens until coated.
3. Arrange lettuce on serving platter.
4. Cut tuna into ½ inch thick slices, coat with ¼ of vinaigrette and arrange atop lettuce.
5. Toss tomatoes, red onion in ¼ of vinaigrette and add on top of the salad.
6. Toss cooked green beans with vinaigrette and add to platter.
7. Finally, arrange hard boiled eggs, olives, and anchovies in mounds on the lettuce bed.
8. Drizzle with remaining dressing, sprinkle entire salad with capers or anchovies (if desired) and serve immediately.

Although traditionally served with potatoes, with a flavorful recipe like this, you'll never realize they're missing!

~ Angela

Seafood Salad Lettuce Wrap

Angela Lewis

Makes 2-4 servings

Ingredients NS

- 4-6 lettuce leaves washed and dried (romaine, iceberg, red or green leaf)
- 7 ½ oz can of wild-caught salmon, shrimp or tuna
- 1 avocado, mashed
- 1-2 hard-boiled eggs, chopped
- 1 tsp extra virgin olive oil
- ⅛ cup diced celery
- ¼ tsp garlic powder
- **¼ tsp paprika** (optional)
- Pinch of tarragon
- Salt & pepper to taste

Directions

1. Mix all ingredients together in bowl, except lettuce leaves.
2. Spoon mixture into individual lettuce leaves.
3. Wrap and enjoy!

Sardine Salad Lettuce Wrap

Chelo Gable

Makes 2 servings

Ingredients NS

- 1 can sardines in olive oil
- 1-2 tsp Dijon mustard to taste
- 1 Tbsp capers
- 1-2 tsp lemon juice to taste
- 4 lettuce leaves (romaine, iceberg, red or green leaf)
- Chopped **tomatoes,** onion and/or avocado (optional)

Directions

1. Combine all ingredients, except lettuce leaves, in a bowl.
2. Portion out an even amount onto 4 lettuce leaves.
3. Fold leaves around mixture and enjoy.

Vegetables & Sides

Broccolini (Spicy Broccoli Rabe)

Jeni Hall

Makes 4-6 servings

Ingredients NS

- ½ cup olive oil
- 2 cloves garlic, sliced
- **½ tsp crushed red pepper flakes**
- 2 bunches of broccolini or broccoli rabe, washed
- Sea salt to taste

Directions

1. Blanch broccolini in salted water for 2 minutes. Drain immediately and immerse in ice bath.
2. Heat oil in a large skillet.
3. Add garlic and crushed red pepper flakes.
4. Add blanched broccolini and mix to coat with oil and garlic.
5. Salt to taste.

Sautéed Swiss Chard

Jeni Hall

Makes 4 servings

Ingredients

- ½ cup coconut oil
- 2 bunches swiss chard, washed and cut
- 2 cloves garlic, crushed
- Salt and pepper to taste

Directions

1. Melt coconut oil in large skillet with a lid.
2. Add greens and toss with the oil.
3. Reduce heat and cover until greens are tender and melted down.
4. Remove lid and add garlic, salt and pepper.
5. Cook on low for ten minutes.

Cauliflower Fried "Rice"

Jeni Hall

Makes 6 servings

Ingredients NS

- 3 Tbsp coconut oil
- 1 head of cauliflower
- 1 small head of broccoli
- **1 red or yellow bell pepper**
- 1 carrot
- 1 onion

- **1-2 jalapeños (optional)**
- 2 Tbsp apple cider vinegar
- 2 tsp toasted sesame oil
- 1 tsp salt
- 2 eggs
- Green onions to garnish

Directions

1. Grate the head of cauliflower and steam for 3 minutes.
2. Chop the broccoli, bell pepper and carrot. Chop onion and jalapeños together and put in a bowl.
3. Lightly scramble the eggs and set aside.
4. Mix toasted sesame oil and vinegar in a bowl and set aside.
5. Heat the coconut oil in a large skillet or wok so that it is very hot but not smoking. Add the grated cauliflower and stir constantly until cauliflower is browned, about 3 minutes.
6. Add the onions and jalapeños. Cook for several minutes until the onions are softened. Add remaining vegetables and saute until they are done.
7. Turn off heat and add eggs to pan, stirring until they finish cooking.
8. Stir in toasted sesame oil and vinegar mixture.
9. Garnish with chopped green onions.

Mushrooms or other vegetables can be added for flavor, color and variety.

~ Jeni

Garlicky Green Beans

Jeni Hall

Makes 4 servings

Ingredients

- 1 lb green beans
- 2 Tbsp ghee
- 2 Tbsp apple cider vinegar
- 2 cloves garlic, crushed

Directions

1. Rinse green beans. Trim ends off of the beans and cut beans into two inch pieces.
2. Steam green beans for approximately 5 minutes or until bright green and crisp.
3. In a bowl, mix ghee and garlic together. Add hot green beans and toss to coat.
4. Add vinegar and salt to taste.
5. Serve hot or cold as a salad.

Brussels Sprouts with Bacon

Jeni Hall

Makes 2 servings

Ingredients

- 2 cups shredded Brussels sprouts
- ½ cup sliced leeks
- 3-4 slices bacon, chopped
- Salt
- Splash of lemon juice

Directions

1. Cook chopped bacon in skillet until evenly cooked. Remove bacon from pan.
2. Cook leeks in hot bacon drippings for 3 minutes.
3. Stir in brussel sprouts and cook for 10 more minutes, stirring often.
4. When vegetables are tender, remove from heat.
5. Add salt to taste and a squeeze of fresh lemon.
6. Sprinkle the bacon pieces on top.

Zucchini Soufflé

Mary Budinger

Makes 4 servings

Ingredients N

- 3 large zucchini
- 2-3 cloves of garlic
- 1 small onion or shallot
- **2 cups raw macadamia nuts**
- 1 tsp sea salt

- Juice from ½ lemon (1 Tbsp)
- ½ cup water
- 3 eggs
- Salt, pepper, parsley
- Coconut oil

Directions

1. Heat the oven to 325 F.
2. Butter a casserole dish big enough to handle 3+ shredded zucchinis.
3. Peel and chop 2-3 cloves of garlic (let them sit for 10 minutes so they may begin their medicinal chemistry before you heat them).
4. Peel and dice 1 small onion (or a shallot).
5. Place macadamia nuts, sea salt, lemon juice and water in food processor and purée until smooth.
6. Put coconut oil in a large skillet and sauté the onions while you shred 3 large zucchinis with a cheese grate.
7. Then add the zucchini and the garlic to the skillet – your goal is to soften the zucchini, about 10 minutes. Drain if there is excess liquid.
8. Get 2 large mixing bowls and 3 eggs. You separate the egg yolks into one bowl, the egg whites into another. Add macadmia nut purée to the yolks, plus salt and pepper, plus parsley, and mix.
9. Beat the eggs whites until they are light and fluffy and hold a peak.
10. Stir ⅓ of the egg whites into the yolk mixture.
11. Add the softened zucchini/onion/garlic into the bowl, stir, and pour all into casserole dish.
12. Fold the rest of the egg whites into the casserole (do not stir – "fold" with a knife to keep it fluffy).
13. Bake about 30 minutes, serve immediately.

> *Julia Childs would probably make this soufflé by first creating a béchamel sauce. This recipe uses different ingredients to achieve a similar creamy texture, without the use of grains or dairy.*
>
> ~ Mary

Zucchini Fritters

Mary Budinger

Makes 4 servings

Ingredients N

- 2 medium zucchini
- 2 eggs
- 1 onion
- **½ cup almond flour** (or 3 Tbsp coconut flour)
- **2 cups raw macadamia nuts**
- 1 tsp sea salt

- Juice from ½ lemon (1 Tbsp)
- ½ cup water
- 1 tsp garlic powder
- 1 tsp sea salt
- 1 tsp pepper
- 1 tsp basil leaf

Directions

1. Preheat oven to 400 F.
2. Grate the zucchini with a cheese grater or food processor.
3. Add the salt and squeeze very tightly with paper towels to get the excess liquid out. Put in a medium sized bowl.
4. Grate the onion and add to the bowl.
5. Place macadamia nuts, sea salt, lemon juice and water in food processor and purée until smooth.
6. Add the eggs, macadamia nut purée and almond flour. Sprinkle the spices on top of the mixture and mix until evenly incorporated.
7. To bake: line a baking sheet with parchment or muffin tins and put tablespoon size amounts of the mixture onto the baking sheet or fill the muffin tins ½ full.
8. Bake for approximately 18-20 minutes or until tops and sides are starting to brown.
9. Serve alone or with homemade ketchup.

Tip

Can also pan fry in coconut oil for a crispier outer coating.

I'm always looking for fun ways to prepare veggies, and this is a kid-favorite at our house. These Zucchini fritters are similar to tater tots or hash browns in taste but are more nutritious. They are also very simple to make and reheat well (and leftovers are great in omelets or with an over-easy egg for breakfast.)

~ Mary

Mashed Cauliflower

Mary Budinger

Makes 4 servings

Ingredients

- 1 small head of cauliflower or bag (16 ounces) frozen cauliflower florets
- 1 garlic clove, crushed (about 1 teaspoon)
- 1 ½ Tbsp coconut oil
- ½ cup coconut milk
- 1 Tbsp plus 2 tsp dried chopped chives
- Salt and black pepper to taste

Directions

1. Cook the cauliflower according to the package directions until it's very soft, but not waterlogged.
2. In a small saucepan, heat the garlic, coconut oil, coconut milk, salt, and pepper, about 1 minute.
3. Meanwhile, purée the cauliflower in the bowl of a food processor, scraping down the sides.
4. Add the coconut milk to the processor, along with 1 Tbsp of chives. Process about 10 seconds.
5. Taste and adjust seasonings. Sprinkle with remaining chives before serving.

Mashed Potatoes are creamy, comforting, delicious... and can be a ticket to the sugar roller coaster, thanks to their direct route over the craggy heights of Insulin Spike Peak. But bow your head in gratitude to the cauliflower. Mashed with some coconut milk, coconut oil, and chives, humble cauliflower provides all the texture and comfort of mashed spuds, without the trip into dangerous territory.

~ Mary

Kale & Brussels Sprout Salad

Mary Budinger

Makes 4 servings

Ingredients

- 1 bunch kale
- 15-20 Brussels sprouts
- 1 medium shallot
- 4 slices nitrate-free bacon
- ½ cup extra virgin olive oil
- ½ cup apple cider vinegar
- 2 Tbsp mustard (no sugar)

Directions

1. In a frying pan, cook bacon until crispy. Set aside to cool.
2. Chop kale, brussel sprouts and shallot into thin slices. Put in a medium bowl.
3. In a small mixing bowl, combine oil, vinegar and mustard. Whisk together.
4. Add the dressing to the salad and toss until mixed.
5. Break bacon into bite size pieces. Top salad with bacon.

Serve with grilled chicken, fish, steak or other protein of your choice.

~ Mary

Coconut Almond Green Beans

Mary Budinger

Makes 4-6 servings

Ingredients NS, N

- 1 Tbsp coconut oil
- **2 Tbsp sliced almonds**
- ½ medium onion, finely diced (about ½ cup)
- 3 cloves garlic, minced (about 1 tablespoon)
- 1 tsp ground cumin
- ½ cup fresh cilantro leaves, minced, ~2 Tbsp (optional)
- **½ tsp red chili pepper flakes**
- 1 tsp ground coriander
- **1 tsp paprika**
- ¾ tsp sea salt
- 1 cup coconut milk
- 1 lb green beans, trimmed
- 1 tsp lime juice

Directions

1. Heat the oil in a large sauté pan over medium heat.
2. Add the almonds and cook until lightly browned. Keep an eye on them; they brown quickly! Transfer almonds to a plate for later. Resist the temptation to eat them!
3. In the same pan, sauté the onion, garlic, cumin, coriander, paprika, chili pepper flakes, and salt. Cook until the onion is soft and beginning to get brown bits, about 4-5 minutes.
4. Add the coconut milk to the pan and mix well, then add the green beans. Make sure everything is blended, then bring the pan to a boil, reduce the heat to a simmer, and cook covered until the beans are tender. Note: The cooking time is a judgment call. If you like them crisp, it's about 6 minutes. If you like them softer, let them braise for about 8 minutes.
5. When the beans have reached the desired tenderness, remove the lid and let the sauce cook down until it thickens a bit.
6. Remove the pan from the heat and stir in the almonds, lime juice, and cilantro

This could become the only green recipe you need. During the braising process, the sliced almonds almost melt into a rich coconut milk sauce that renders the elements indistinguishable from each other. And that's when you know the ingredients have fulfilled their destiny. Trust me: make a double batch.

~ Mary

Oven Roasted Vegetables

Heather Page

Makes 4-6 servings

ingredients NS

- 1 large red onion, cut into 1 inch pieces
- 2 medium parsnips, peeled and cut into 1 inch pieces
- 2 carrots, peeled and cut into 1 inch pieces
- 12 Brussels sprouts, trimmed and sliced in half
- 1 large turnip or beet, cut into 1 inch pieces
- **1 red, yellow or orange bell pepper, cored and cut into 1 inch pieces**

Other Ingredients

- ¼ cup olive oil or coconut oil, melted
- ½ tsp rosemary
- 1 tsp thyme
- ½ tsp marjoram
- 1-2 cloves garlic, crushed
- 1 tsp sea salt
- Fresh ground pepper to taste

Directions

1. Mix herbs, garlic, sea salt and pepper with coconut or olive oil. Set aside.
2. Place vegetables in large bowl. Pour oil/seasoning mixture over vegetables and toss well to coat evenly.
3. Spread coated vegetables onto rimmed and parchment-lined baking sheet.
4. Bake at 375 F for 15 minutes. Stir veggies and bake for another 10-15 minutes (25-30 total, or until firm, but tender).

Grandma's Red Cabbage

Jennifer Konow

Makes 6-8 servings

Ingredients F

- 1 large yellow onion, sliced
- 1 head of small cabbage, shredded
- **2 green apples, sliced**
- 5 Tbsp of apple cider vinegar
- 2 Tbsp of rosemary
- 2 Tbsp of coconut oil or lard

Directions

1. Sauté the onion with the oil or fat on medium heat.
2. Add cabbage when onions become translucent.
3. Add the rosemary, apple cider vinegar and apples, and sauté until the cabbage softens.

A Dutch Oven works great for this recipe.
~ Jennifer

Kale Salad

Tara Chatterton

Makes 4-6 servings

Ingredients F

- 1 bunch of Tuscan kale - de-stemmed and minced
- ½ cabbage minced in food processor
- **½ green apple - tiny slices**
- 4 small steamed beets-cut in small pieces
- bunch of chopped green olives
- ½ small red onion
- 1 knob of ginger
- 1 clove garlic

Dressing

- 1 tsp sea salt - to taste
- 3-4 Tbsp of olive oil
- 2 Tbsp Apple Cider vinegar or lemon juice (optional)

Directions

1. Prepare the kale by removing all stems. Chop the kale, then put it in the food processor to cut it up finer, while still leaving some bite size pieces.

2. Cut the red cabbage in small chunks and mince in food processor. This adds more crunch to the salad.

3. Mince the onion, ginger, and garlic, and lightly pan fry in olive oil on medium heat.

4. Cut the apple and beets in slices, then smaller pieces.

5. Chop olives in small pieces.

6. Combine all prepared salad ingredients in a bowl.

7. Mix the dressing and toss with the kale salad mix.

Believe it or not, I don't eat much kale, my dogs eat more kale than I do in their raw food diet. I like kale... sometimes, but feel that most kale salads are a hit or miss, so I have been reluctant to create my own. After a few not so great attempts, I finally came up with this simple, but flavorful recipe and it was a big hit!

~ Tara

Creamy Zucchini Noodles

Jessica Kouka

Makes 4 servings

Ingredients N, NS

- Olive Oil
- 2 medium zucchini, shredded into "noodles" (with julienne peeler, mandolin slicer, spiralizer etc.)
- **¾ cup cashews**
- 2 cloves garlic, minced or pressed
- **1 Tbsp tahini (sesame paste)**
- 1 tsp sea salt
- Juice of 1 small lemon
- Dash of nutmeg
- 1 Tbsp Brewer's or nutritional yeast
- 4 fresh basil leaves, chopped
- **1 cup cherry tomatoes, halved**

Directions

1. Soak cashews for 2-4 hours in water, discard water and grind up in food processor.
2. Shred zucchini into noodles.
3. Mix all ingredients except basil and tomatoes.
4. Grease saucepan with olive oil and heat to medium-low.
5. Add zucchini mixture and top with lid.
6. Cook until just heated through or until zucchini reaches desired softness (add a few spoonfuls of water if cooking longer).
7. Remove from heat and top with tomatoes and basil. Serve.

This recipe can be served raw without heating. This dish is so creamy you will have people thinking it is full of butter, cheese, and cream!

~ Jessica

Beet Salad

Mary Budinger

Makes 4 servings

Ingredients N, F

- 1 bunch red or yellow beets
- 1 Tbsp coconut oil, melted
- **⅓ cup shelled pistachios**
- **Juice of ¼ grapefruit (about 2 tsp)**
- 1 Tbsp red wine vinegar
- 1 clove garlic, minced (about 1 tsp)
- ⅛ tsp salt

- ⅛ tsp ground cumin
- ⅛ tsp ground coriander
- ⅛ tsp ground cinnamon
- A few shakes of ground black pepper
- 2 Tbsp extra virgin olive oil
- 2 scallions, white and green, thinly sliced (about ¼ cup)

Directions

1. Wash the beets, and cut off the stem and root ends. Cut the beets in half. Toss them in a pan of gently boiling water for about 30 minutes. Then take them out of the pan, let them start to cool, peel off the skins, and cube them. TIP: Use parchment paper on top of your cutting board for easier cleanup—beets tend to stain.

2. To toast the pistachios, toss them in coconut oil and spread them in a single layer on a baking sheet. Bake for 20-30 minutes at 325°F.

3. Whisk the grapefruit juice, vinegar, cumin, coriander, cinnamon, garlic, salt, and pepper in a small bowl. Whisking continuously, drizzle in the olive oil and then set aside.

4. Coarsely chop the pistachios and set aside.

5. Place the beets in a large bowl and toss with the dressing. Add the scallions and pistachios and toss well with two wooden spoons.

6. Allow to cool to room temperature before eating.

7. Add salt and pepper, to taste.

Create-a-Salad

Kariman Pierce

Makes 1 serving

Ingredients NS, N

- Greens (green leaf, red leaf, romaine, spinach, arugula etc.)
- Fresh herbs-mint, basil, rosemary etc.
- Carrots
- Cucumbers
- Celery
- **Tomatoes**
- Radishes
- **Bell peppers**
- Sprouts
- Roasted Root Vegetables - beet, parsnips, turnips, rutabaga, celery root

- Hard-boiled eggs
- Avocado
- **Raw or Dry Roasted Nuts & Seeds — pistachios, pecans, slivered almonds, walnuts, macadamia nuts, brazil nuts, sesame seeds, sunflower seeds**
- Sauerkraut
- Chicken, Beef, Pork, Fish — shredded, ground or chopped
- Bacon
- Sardines
- Dressing of your choice (pp. 84-90)

Directions

1. Prep 2 large handfuls (per person) of greens and place in medium or large size bowl.
2. Choose 2-4 raw vegetables, chop to desired size and add to bowl.
3. Choose 1-2 soft or cooked vegetable (hint, root vegetables or avocado?).
4. Choose a protein and add.
5. Choose any other ingredients for texture, color and flavor.
6. Toss with salad dressing and enjoy!

Open up your fridge and pull out greens and leftovers. Then grab another 2-4 veggies for a great salad. A great lunch is often leftovers turned into a salad which is so easy to make and take to work. Yum!

~ Kariman

Aunt Karin's Ginger Carrots

Jennifer Konow

Makes 4-6 servings

Ingredients

- 4 cups diced carrots
- 2 Tbsp coconut oil
- 1 knob shredded fresh ginger

Directions

1. Use a food processor or cut carrots into coin size.
2. Shred ginger with grater.
3. Put coconut oil in dutch oven or saucier pan and bring up to medium heat.
4. Place carrots and shredded ginger in pan and put lid on.
5. Stir every few minutes until soft.

Creamy Coconut Kale

Heather Page

Makes 2 servings

Ingredients

- 2 Tbsp coconut oil
- ½ yellow onion, finely diced
- 1 2" knob fresh ginger, minced
- 1 10 oz. pkg baby kale
- 1 cup coconut milk
- Salt and pepper to taste

Directions

1. Heat the oil in a large skillet on medium. Add the ginger and onion and sauté for 5 minutes.
2. Add the kale and sauté, stirring constantly for another minute.
3. Add the coconut milk, salt and pepper.
4. Bring to a boil. Reduce heat and simmer until kale is tender and sauce is reduced. Serve in shallow bowl.

 **RESTART**

Broths & Soups

Kristi's Cream of Celery Soup

Kariman Pierce (recipe from a RESTART® student)

Makes 4 servings

Ingredients NS, N

- 2 Tbsp ghee for sauté
- 1 large onion, diced
- 3-4 garlic cloves, minced
- 2 bunches of celery, chopped
- 4 cups mild broth of choice (preferably homemade)
- **1 cup Basic Cashew Cream/Milk** (p. 119)

- 1 bay leaf
- ½ tsp dried oregano
- 1 tsp sea salt
- 1-2 Tbsp fresh lemon juice (to taste)
- Scallions for garnish
- **Dash of smoked paprika (optional)**

Directions

1. Saute onions in ghee on medium heat until translucent, 5-10 minutes.
2. Add garlic and continue to sauté a minute more.
3. Add celery and sauté another 10 minutes.
4. Add broth, bay leaf, oregano and sea salt.
5. Bring to a boil and then immediately reduce to a simmer.
6. Simmer for 15-20 minutes (or until celery is soft) on low with pot partially covered.
7. Remove 1 cup of vegetables (strain liquid) and set aside to add back later. (This is optional)
8. Take out bay leaf and toss.
9. Transfer all contents of the pot to a blender and process or blend until smooth.
10. With the stove on the lowest setting, return soup to pot, add cashew cream, lemon juice and reserved veggies for texture.
11. Garnish with scallions, dash of smoked paprika.

Use a high powered blender for best soup consistency.

~ Kariman

Creamy Cauliflower Soup

Jeni Hall

Makes 8 servings

Ingredients NS

- 1 Tbsp ghee
- 1 head cauliflower, chopped
- 2 leeks, white only, cleaned and chopped
- 2 quarts chicken bone broth
- **1 tsp curry powder**
- Salt and pepper to taste
- Cilantro and **paprika** for garnish

Directions

1. Saute leeks in ghee, salt, pepper and curry powder.
2. Add remaining ingredients and cook until vegetables are soft.
3. Puree.
4. Garnish with cilantro and paprika.

Carrot Ginger Soup

Mary Budinger

Makes 8 servings

Ingredients

- 1 Tbsp ghee or clarified butter
- 4 shallots, minced
- 2 Tbsp fresh ginger, peeled and grated
- 2 quarts chicken broth
- 2 cups coconut milk, optional
- Salt and pepper to taste
- 3 lbs carrots, grated
- Fresh parsley for garnish

Directions:

1. Saute shallots in ghee with salt and pepper.
2. Add remaining ingredients and cook until vegetables are soft.
3. Puree, adding more broth or water if necessary.
4. Garnish with parsley.

Chicken & Winter Vegetable Soup

Makes 6-8 servings

Ingredients

- 3 large carrots, peeled
- 1 large turnip, peeled
- 1 large parsnip, peeled
- 1 large celery root, peeled
- 1 large beet, peeled
- 2 Tbsp olive oil
- Salt to taste
- Pepper to taste
- Thyme to taste
- 4 chicken leg quarters
- 6 to 8 cups chicken stock

Directions

1. Preheat oven at 425 F.
2. On a parchment-lined cookie sheet, place 4 leg quarters, salt and pepper and place in the hot oven to start cooking. Roast for 40 minutes or until thouroughly cooked.
3. Dice all the vegetables into 1 to 1 ½ inch cubes. Place all the cut vegetables in a single layer on a large parchment-lined cookie sheet pan. Drizzle them with olive oil, thyme, salt and pepper. Toss well and bake for 25 minutes, or until the vegetables are tender, turning once with a spatula.
4. In a large saucepan heat 6 cups of chicken stock.
5. When the vegetables are done roasting, puree them in a food processor.
6. Add the puree to the stock.
7. Scrape any oil that is remaining in the cookie sheet and add to the soup.
8. Adjust the seasoning with salt and pepper to your liking.
9. Serve in a large soup bowl.
10. Cut the chicken in small bite-sized pieces and place in the middle of the soup.
11. Serve nice and hot.

Sausage, Cabbage & Root Vegetable Soup

Jennifer Steakley

Makes 8-10 servings

Ingredients

- 1 lb breakfast pan sausage (no sugar added)
- 1-2 Tbsp coconut oil
- ½ head cabbage chopped
- 2 large turnips cubed
- 3 medium/large parsnips chopped
- 8-10 cups Homemade Bone Broth (pp. 81-82)
- 4-5 cloves garlic grated
- 1 Tbsp sea salt
- ½ tsp pepper
- 3-4 sprigs fresh rosemary

Directions

1. Brown sausage in large stock pot or dutch oven with coconut oil.
2. Add remaining ingredients to the pot. Bring to a boil over medium high heat, then reduce heat to medium low/low and simmer until root vegetables are cooked.

Remove rosemary stems before eating.
~ Jennifer

Beef & Cauliflower Soup

Mary Budinger

Makes 8 servings

Ingredients NS

- 1 lb grass-fed hamburger
- ½ cup chopped onion
- 2 cloves minced garlic
- 1 Tbsp apple cider vinegar
- **1 14.5-ounce can crushed tomatoes**
- ⅓ cup riced cauliflower
- 1 cup sliced carrots

- ¾ cup chopped celery
- ¼ tsp black pepper
- ½ tsp oregano
- ½ tsp basil
- 1 bay leaf
- Coconut oil or ghee
- 2 cups water

Optional Ingredients

- 2 cups chopped washed greens, such as spinach, kale, or Swiss chard
- 2 cups sliced mushrooms

Directions

1. Coat large Dutch oven with coconut oil or ghee. Place Dutch oven on stove over medium high heat.
2. Add ground beef. Stir to crumble while browning.
3. Add onion and garlic to meat. Cook onion and garlic until translucent.
4. Add apple cider vinegar, crushed tomatoes, water, shredded cauliflower, carrots, celery and spices.
5. Bring to a boil, reduce heat to a simmer, and cover.
6. Simmer until vegetables are done (about 30 minutes).
7. Add optional vegetables.
8. Return to a simmer for about 8-12 minutes.
9. Taste for salt and serve.

A word about Bone Broth
Aypril Porter

Bone broth is a very nourishing, traditional food. Our ancestors honored the animals they ate by utilizing them, nose to tail. They ate every part including the muscles and fat, and savored the highly nutritious organ meats. They used the bones for making broth. Intuitively, they knew of the healing power of broth and found that the liquid provided support for joints, skin, hair, nails, and healing of the intestinal lining.

Bone Broth and Vinegar
Aypril Porter

In the following recipes, vinegar is in the ingredients list. The vinegar will not be tasted in the final product. It is a critical ingredient in the process as it helps to pull the minerals from the bones into the broth.

If desired, add more water and apple cider vinegar to the bones in the crock and make another batch.

Additionally, you can add vegetable scraps to your broth for more flavor, like celery, carrot, onion, etc. Spices are another great addition if you like. Pepper, turmeric, etc.

Beef Bone Broth

Aypril Porter

Yields approximately 2 quarts

Ingredients

- 3-5 lbs bones (use organic or grass-fed bones from healthy animals)
- Filtered water
- 1 Tbsp raw apple cider vinegar
- Vegetable scraps-onion, carrot, celery, etc.
- Spices-pepper, turmeric, etc.

Directions

1. When making a beef bone broth, combine marrow bones with knuckles/joints and/or soup bones for the most gelatinous rich broth.

2. Roast bones in oven at 350 F on a baking sheet for about 40 minutes or until they start to brown.

3. Remove bones from the oven and place in a large crock pot. Fill with filtered water and add 1 Tbsp raw apple cider vinegar. Set to high until water begins to simmer, then turn to low heat and leave simmering for the next 24-72 hours. Longer cook times can increase amount of histamines in broth, so opt for a shorter cook time if this is an issue for you.

4. After about 24 hours, check broth. If it looks rich and to your liking, turn temperature off and let cool for about 30 min.

5. Strain through a fine mesh colander or cheese cloth to remove and large pieces of bone or meat if you desire a more filtered broth.

6. Store in glass jars to finish cooling and place in refrigerator. Transfer to storage bags or containers for freezing after completely chilled.

7. Steps 3-6 can be repeated using the same bones a couple more times to make more broth. The first batch will have the most flavor, so use that for drinking, and save the later batches for soups, or in place of water when cooking grains/seeds like quinoa.

Chicken Bone Broth

Aypril Porter

Yields approximately 2 quarts

Ingredients

- Whole chicken
- Filtered water
- 1 Tbsp raw apple cider vinegar

- Vegetable scraps-onion, carrot, celery, etc.
- Spices-pepper, turmeric, etc. (optional)

Directions

1. Clean whole chicken and remove gizzards, neck, etc from internal cavity.
2. Roast chicken either in oven or crock pot.
3. Remove chicken meat and set aside for other meals.
4. Place all bones, cartilage, skin and neck into the crock pot. Add optional vegetables and spices.
5. Cover with filtered water, add raw apple cider vinegar, and set to high until water begins to simmer, then turn to Cook for 12-18 hours.
6. Turn off heat, and let cool.
7. Strain through a fine mesh colander or cheese cloth to remove and large pieces of bone or meat if you desire a more filtered broth.
8. Store in glass jars to finish cooling and place in refrigerator.
   Transfer to storage bags or containers for freezing after completely chilled.
9. Steps 5-9 can be repeated using the same bones a couple more times to make more broth. The first batch will have the most flavor, so use that for drinking, and save the later batches for soups, or in place of water when cooking grains/seeds like quinoa.

Sauces, Dressings, & Dips

Creamy Avocado Dressing

Jennifer Steakley

Makes 8 servings

Ingredients

- ½ can full fat coconut milk
- 1 whole avocado
- 1 Tbsp raw apple cider vinegar
- ⅛ tsp pepper
- ½ tsp salt

Directions

1. Blend all ingredients together.
2. Thin with a little water if desired.
3. Use immediately. Does not do well for leftovers.

Ranch Dressing

Jeni Hall

Makes 6 servings

Ingredients

- 1 cup Basic Mayonnaise (p. 91)
- 1 Tbsp minced parsley
- 1 Tbsp chives or scallions
- 1 clove crushed garlic
- ¼ tsp sea salt
- Squeeze of lemon
- Salt and pepper to taste

Directions

1. Combine all ingredients.
2. Chill before serving.

Thousand Island Dressing

Mary Budinger

Makes 6-8 servings

Ingredients NS

- 1 cup Basic Mayonnaise (p. 91)
- **3 Tbsp chili sauce**
- 2 green onions, finely chopped
- **1 Tbsp finely diced bell pepper**
- 1 large hard cooked egg white, chopped

Directions

1. Place all ingredients in a blender jar and blend for 8 seconds.
2. Refrigerate for up to 10 days.
3. Makes 1 ¼ cups.

Creamy Garlic Dressing

Mary Budinger

Makes 12 servings

Ingredients

- 2 cups Basic Mayonnaise (p. 91)
- 6 cloves of minced garlic
- ½ tsp Herbes de Provence
- Pinch of sea salt and a dash of pepper

Directions

1. Place all ingredients in a jar and shake vigorously.
2. Refrigerate for 6 hours before serving to bring out the garlic flavor.
3. Makes 2 cups.

Mary's Simplest Dressing

Mary Budinger

Makes 4 servings

Ingredients

- Equal parts olive oil and balsamic vinegar
- Dollop of mustard
- Dash of basil or other herbs, if feeling adventurous

Directions

1. Place all ingredients in a glass jar and blend or shake vigorously.
2. No need to refrigerate.

Broth Vinaigrette Dressing

Mary Budinger

Makes 4-6 servings

Ingredients

- ½ cup chicken broth
- 1 Tbsp mustard
- 2 Tbsp extra virgin olive oil
- 1 Tbsp lemon juice

Directions

1. Place all ingredients in a jar and shake vigorously.
2. Refrigerate.
3. Makes about ¾ cup.

Walnut Dressing

Mary Budinger

Makes 4 servings

Ingredients

- 2 Tbsp apple cider vinegar
- **2 Tbsp unrefined walnut oil**
- 6 Tbsp olive oil
- 1 handful of walnuts

Directions

1. Place in blender and blend for 10 seconds — this will leave some chunks of nuts.
2. Refrigerate. You can serve additional walnut pieces on salad.

Basic Italian Vinaigrette

Jeni Hall

Makes 12 servings

Ingredients

- 1 ½ cup extra virgin olive oil
- 1 tsp dried oregano
- ½ cup apple cider vinegar
- 2 tsp dried parsley
- 2-4 cloves of garlic
- Salt and pepper to taste

Directions

1. Blend all ingredients together in a blender until smooth.
2. Refrigerate overnight to enhance flavors.

Lemon Vinaigrette

Nancy Sullivan

Makes 4 servings

Ingredients

- 2 Tbsp lemon juice, unstrained
- Black pepper to taste
- 6 Tbsp olive oil
- $\frac{1}{8}$ tsp mustard
- Scant tsp sea salt
- 4-6 cloves of garlic, crushed

Directions

1. Place all ingredients in a jar and shake vigorously.
2. Refrigerate.

Olive Oil-Avocado Dressing

Hollis Baley

Makes 6-8 servings

Ingredients

- 1 avocado
- 2 tsp apple cider vinegar
- $\frac{1}{4}$ cup organic extra virgin olive oil
- $\frac{1}{4}$ tsp sea salt
- $\frac{1}{3}$ cup filtered water

Directions

1. Mix all ingredients in a blender or food processor until smooth.
2. Add water if necessary to thin.
3. Refrigerate. Best to use immediately or within a couple days.

Citrus-Avocado Dressing

Hollis Baley

Makes 6-8 servings

Ingredients F

- 1 avocado
- **⅓ cup fresh squeezed grapefruit juice**
- 2-3 Tbsp fresh squeezed lemon juice
- ⅓ cup organic extra-virgin olive oil
- ¼ filtered water
- 1 tsp apple cider vinegar
- ¼ tsp ginger powder
- ¼ tsp sea salt

Directions:

1. Mix all ingredients in a blender or food processor until smooth.
2. Refrigerate. Best to use immediately or within a couple of days.

Guacamole

Heather Page

Makes 4 servings

Ingredients NS

- 2 ripe avocados, peeled and pitted
- 1-2 Tbsp fresh squeezed lime juice
- 2 Tbsp fresh cilantro, chopped
- **1 roma tomato, diced**
- **½ jalapeño, seeded and minced**
- ¼ cup red onion, minced
- Salt and pepper to taste

Directions:

1. Mash avocado, lime juice and salt in bowl. Add in jalapeño, tomato, cilantro, red onion and pepper and mix until desired texture.
2. Refrigerate. Best to use immediately or within a couple of days.

Creamy Cashew Dressing/Spread/Dip

Jessica Kouka

Makes 6 servings

Ingredients N, NS

- 1 cup fresh parsley sprigs
- **½ cup cashews (soaked 4 hours and drained)**
- 2 sprigs green onion
- 1 clove garlic
- 2 Tbsp olive oil
- 2 Tbsp balsamic vinegar
- 2 Tbsp fresh lemon juice
- Salt, pepper, and/or **red pepper flakes** to taste

Directions

1. Place all ingredients in blender and blend until smooth.
   This makes a thick and creamy dressing which can also be used as a spread or dip.
2. Add more liquid ingredients (olive oil, vinegar) for a thinner dressing, or add more cashews for a thicker spread.

> *You can play around with the ingredients! Add another clove of garlic if a strong garlic flavor is desired. Use cilantro or basil instead of parsley. You won't miss dairy with this creamy sauce, and guests will be asking you for your recipe!*
>
> *~ Jessica*

Hollandaise Sauce

Jeni Hall

Makes 4 servings

Ingredients

- 3 yolks from large eggs
- 1 - 1 ½ Tbsp fresh lemon juice
- ½ cup ghee

Directions

1. Mix eggs and lemon in medium saucepan away from stove.
2. Add ¼ cup of ghee and whisk constantly over low to medium heat.
3. When melted, add remaining ¼ cup of ghee and continue to whisk until sauce begins to thicken.
4. Serve immediately.

Basic Mayonnaise

Jeni Hall

Makes 8 servings

Ingredients N

- 1 cup oil - olive, high oleic **sunflower**, **walnut** or avocado
- 1 egg
- 2 Tbsp lemon juice
- 1 tsp mustard - yellow, brown or dijon
- Sea salt and pepper

Directions

1. Place all ingredients except oil in food processor or hand blender.
2. Turn on food processor/hand blender and drizzle oil in slowly until thoroughly blended.

Red Palm Oil Garlic Spread/Mayonnaise

Tara Chatterton

Yields 1 1/4 cups

Ingredients

- 2 eggs
- 1 Tbsp apple cider vinegar
- Juice of ½ a lemon
- 1 Tbsp sea salt
- ¾ cup olive oil
- ¼ cup red palm oil
- 2-3 minced garlic cloves

Directions

1. Mix eggs, vinegar, lemon juice, and sea salt with an emulsion/hand blender.
2. Add minced garlic.
3. Then drizzle olive oil is slowly while blending to give it time to emulsify and not separate.
4. Next slowly add the red palm oil. The mixture will turn a bright yellow.
5. Put in the fridge which will thicken it further.

This recipe is less bitter than using olive oil alone and has a better consistency. Because of the thickness of red palm oil, it won't harden as much as coconut oil. It is thick enough for spreading or dipping. It is a good choice to mix into chicken or tuna salad.

~ Tara

Basic Ketchup

Kariman Pierce

Yields approximately 3 cups

Ingredients NS, F

- **1 (12 ounce) can tomato paste**
- **½ cup juiced green apple**
- 1 Tbsp distilled white vinegar
- ¾ cup cold water
- **1 tsp paprika**
- ½ tsp salt
- ¼ tsp ground thyme
- ¼ tsp garlic powder
- ⅛ tsp onion powder
- ⅛ tsp ground allspice
- 1⅛ tsp ground cumin

Directions

1. Combine all ingredients in a stock pot. Bring to a boil stirring frequently until the mixture has reduced by half.
2. Pour into a container with a lid and refrigerate until using. Use or freeze within 1 week.

Creamy Coconut-Basil Pesto

Hollis Baley

Yields 1 1/2 cups

Ingredients N

- ¼ cup full fat coconut milk (unsweetened)
- ¼ cup filtered water
- 2 cups fresh basil
- 2-3 cloves garlic
- ½ cup organic extra-virgin olive oil
- 2-3 Tbsp fresh lemon juice
- **¼ cup pine-nuts, walnuts, or pecans (optional)**
- 1 tsp fresh ginger juice (optional)
- Sea salt to taste

Directions

1. Place all ingredients into a blender and blend until desired consistency is reached.
2. Refrigerate.

Works great as a garnish for meat and vegetable dishes. Also makes an easy "go-to" as a fresh vegetable dipping sauce.

~ Hollis

Pico de Gallo
Heather Page

Yields 2 cups

Ingredients NS

- **2 medium tomatoes, diced**
- ½ yellow onion, finely diced
- **1 small jalapeño, seeded and finely diced**
- 3 cloves garlic, minced
- ¼ cup cilantro, chopped
- Juice of 1 lime
- Unrefined sea salt

Directions

1. Mix all ingredients together
2. Salt to taste.
3. Can be served immediately or refrigerated for a few hours.

This is a great topping for lettuce wrap tacos, burgers or even fish. Can also serve with guacamole as a dip for vegetables.

~ Heather

Taco Seasoning
Jennifer Steakley

Yields 1 cup

Ingredients NS

- **½ cup chili powder**
- 1 Tbsp garlic powder
- ¼ cup onion powder
- **1 Tbsp paprika**
- ⅛ cup ground cumin
- 1 Tbsp sea salt

Directions

1. Mix well in small bowl.
2. Store in jar.

Italian Seasoning
Heather Page

Yields 1 cup

Ingredients

- 3 Tbsp oregano
- 3 Tbsp basil
- 3 Tbsp thyme
- 3 Tbsp marjoram
- 2 Tbsp rosemary
- 1 Tbsp + 1 tsp sage

Directions

1. Mix well in small bowl.
2. Store in jar.

Anytime Treats

Bacon Pancakes

Mary Budinger

Makes 6 Small pancakes

Ingredients

- 6 slices of bacon
- 3 eggs
- ¼ cup coconut flour
- 1 Tbsp purified granular gelatin
- 2 Tbsp butter or ghee, melted
- 2 Tbsp finely chopped chives
- ½ cup water

Directions

1. Cook the bacon in a frying pan over medium heat. Leave the bacon fat in the pan. Crumble or finely chop the bacon and set aside.
2. If just egg whites, whisk into soft peaks. If whole eggs, separate the yolks from the whites and whisk the whites. Mix the egg yolks together in a separate bowl. Set aside.
3. In a large bowl, mix together the coconut flour, gelatin, butter, chives, bacon, and egg yolks. Add the water and mix well, then gently fold in the egg whites until combined. The batter will be thick and lumpy.
4. Re-heat the bacon fat in the frying pan over medium heat.
5. Scoop small amounts (about 2 tablespoons) of batter into the pan, gently smoothing the batter out with a spoon to form small pancakes. Cook about 3 minutes on each side. Serve warm.

This recipe uses gelatin. Why add gelatin to pancakes? Because you can, without affecting the flavor or texture! Gelatin, the same thing that makes beef broth so healthful, can benefit bone, joint, and skin health, and improve sleep.

~ Mary

Zucchini Almond Pancakes

Mary Budinger

Makes 10-12 pancakes

Ingredients N

- 4 large organic eggs
- 3 cups grated zucchini
- **¾-1 cup almond flour**
- ½ cup minced onion
- ½-1 tsp sea salt
- freshly ground black pepper
- butter or ghee for cooking

Directions

1. Mix all ingredients except the ghee together in a medium-sized bowl. Batter will thin a little as it sits.

2. Heat a 10-inch stainless steel or cast iron skillet over medium-low heat. Be sure to heat your pan long enough before adding the ghee and batter, otherwise the pancakes will stick.

3. Add about one tablespoon ghee. Drop batter by the ¼-cup into the hot skillet. Cook for a few minutes on each side. Repeat with remaining batter, adding ghee or butter to the skillet before cooking each pancake.

A well-seasoned cast iron skillet or a ceramic pan keeps pancakes from sticking to the bottom of the pan and is especially useful in this recipe.

~ Mary

2-Ingredient Pancakes

Jeni Hall

Makes 1-2 servings

Ingredients F

- **1 green-tipped banana**
- 1-2 eggs
- Coconut oil, butter or ghee (for frying)

Directions

1. Blend together until smooth.
2. Heat fat of choice in pan.
3. Pan fry until golden brown.
4. Serve with butter or ghees, cinnamon, toasted coconut, berries, etc.

Banana Nut Butter Pancakes

Makes 4 small pancakes

Ingredients N, F

- **1 green-tipped banana**
- 1 pastured egg
- **2 Tbsp almond butter**
- Dash of cinnamon
- Coconut oil to fry

Directions

1. Preheat skillet over medium heat.
2. Whisk egg in a small bowl.
3. Add banana and smash with fork.
4. Add almond butter and cinnamon and stir until well blended.
5. Grease skillet with coconut oil. Add drops of batter to form 3-4 inch pancakes. Fry on both sides, about 2 minutes each side.

 **RESTART®**

Warm Chia & Hemp "Cereal"

Jessica Bischof

Makes 1 serving

Ingredients N

- ½ cup unsweetened **almond** or coconut milk, warmed
- **1-2 Tbsp chia seeds**
- **2 Tbsp hemp seeds**
- 1 pat butter or ghee
- Dash of sea salt
- ¼ tsp nutmeg or cinnamon

Directions

1. Mix all ingredients except butter into warm milk.
2. Add butter or ghee to the top.
3. Let ingredients sit 5-10 minutes until chia is swollen. Stir and enjoy!

This works well in a glass pint jar for an on the go breakfast.

~ Jessica

Apple, Cinnamon, Ginger Muffins

Mary Budinger

Makes 8-10 muffins

Ingredients N, F

- 2 Tbsp organic coconut oil
- **½ cup finely diced Granny Smith apples**
- 1 tsp ground cinnamon
- ½ tsp ground ginger
- **2 cups almond meal**
- ¼ tsp sea salt
- ½ tsp baking soda
- 3 large organic pasture-raised eggs
- 2 Tbsp organic extra-virgin coconut oil
- ½ Tbsp freshly squeezed lemon juice
- ½ Tbsp water
- 1 tsp vanilla extract

Directions

1. Heat oven 350 F. Line a muffin pan with muffin papers.
2. Cook apples until soft in a skillet in coconut oil. Remove from heat and add the cinnamon and ginger. Stir until well coated and allow to cool while making batter.
3. Mix the dry ingredients in one bowl.
4. In another bowl whisk together the eggs, coconut oil, lemon juice, water and vanilla. Combine dry and wet ingredients until well blended. Stir in apple mixture. Fill each muffin cup ¾ full with batter and bake for 13-15 minutes or until toothpick comes out dry.

Rosemary & Banana-Nut Muffins

Hollis Baley

Makes 8-10 muffins

Ingredients N, F

- **2 cups almond meal/flour**
- ½ tsp sea salt
- ¼ tsp fresh ground pepper
- ½ tsp baking soda
- 3 large organic pasture-raised eggs
- ½ tsp organic extra-virgin coconut oil
- ½ Tbsp fresh squeezed lemon juice
- ½ Tbsp filtered water
- **1 green-tipped banana cut into small squares**
- 3 Tbsp chopped **walnuts, pecans, or almonds** (optional)
- 1 ½ tsp finely chopped rosemary

Directions

1. Preheat oven to 350 F. Line muffin tin with muffin papers.
2. Mix dry ingredients together in one bowl.
3. Mix eggs, coconut oil, lemon juice, bananas and water together in another bowl.
4. Blend dry and wet ingredients. Stir in nuts and rosemary.
5. Fill each muffin cup ¾ full with batter and bake for 12-15 minutes or until a toothpick comes out clean. Enjoy alone or with organic pasture-raised butter or ghee.

Banana Muffins

Heather Page

Makes 10 muffins

Ingredients F

- 5 pastured eggs
- **2 green tipped bananas**
- ½ cup unsweetened coconut flakes
- ¼ cup coconut oil (melted and cooled)
- ½ cup coconut flour
- 1 tsp baking soda
- ¼ tsp salt
- 1 tsp vanilla
- ¼ cup coconut milk
- 1 tsp cinnamon (optional)

Directions

1. Preheat oven to 400 F.
2. Put all ingredients in medium sized bowl.
3. Using a hand mixer, mix until smooth and well incorporated.
   OR put all ingredients in blender for a smoother mixture.
4. Scoop into parchment lined muffin tins- Use a ⅓ cup measure to make even sized. Batter will be somewhat thick.
5. Bake for 15-20 minutes until lightly browned and set in middle.

Almond Spice Muffins

Kariman Pierce

Makes 12 muffins

Ingredients N, F

- **1 cup creamy almond butter (check ingredient list for added sugars!)**
- 4 eggs
- **1 green tipped banana, mashed**
- 2 tsp vanilla extract
- ½ tsp sea salt
- ½ tsp baking soda
- 2 Tbsp of pumpkin pie spice (or cinnamon)
- 12 baking cups

Directions

1. Preheat oven to 325 F.
2. In a large mixing bowl blend together almond butter, eggs, banana and vanilla extract with a hand mixer.
3. Add sea salt, baking soda and spice and blend until well combined.
4. Pour batter into baking cups.
5. Bake for 20 minutes.

3 muffins equal daily RESTART® allotment of nuts (equal to 4 Tbsp of nut butter)

~ Kariman

Banana "Ice Cream"
Jeni Hall

Makes 2 servings

Ingredients F

- **1-2 frozen green-tipped bananas (peel before freezing)**
- 2-4 Tbsp of coconut cream (optional)

Directions

1. Blend in food processor.
2. Add shredded coconut, nuts, etc., as a topping.

Blueberry Cream

Bev Alam

Makes 4-6 servings

Ingredients F

- 1 can coconut milk (refrigerated overnight)
- **1 cup blueberries**
- 1 lemon juiced
- 1 tsp pure vanilla extract
- ¼ tsp cinnamon

Directions

1. In a large bowl place berries, lemon juice, vanilla extract and cinnamon.
2. Add the cream off the top of the canned coconut milk (use the coconut water left behind for another recipe or add to smoothies).
3. With a standing mixer or hand mixer beat the coconut cream, breaking up some berries and combining other ingredients.
4. Serve and enjoy!

This can be eaten as part of breakfast or as dessert.

~ Bev

Toasted Coconut Flakes with Cinnamon & Himalayan Sea Salt

Heather Page

Makes 16 servings

Ingredients

- 4 cups organic coconut flakes
- 1 ½ tsp cinnamon
- ¼ - ½ tsp himalayan salt

Directions

1. Preheat oven to 325 F.
2. Spread coconut flakes on parchment lined baking sheets.
3. Bake for 15-20 minutes, checking every few minutes (check closely at end as they will burn quickly), until golden brown.
4. Remove from oven and sprinkle cinnamon and salt over while still hot.
5. Toss in bowl and add more cinnamon and salt as desired.
6. Serve when cooled.
7. Store any remaining in air tight container and refrigerate.

Sautéed Green Apple with Cinnamon

Heather Page

Makes 2 servings

Ingredients F, N

- 2 Tbsp coconut oil
- **1 green apple**
- ½ tsp cinnamon
- **Almond Butter** and unsweetened coconut flakes as toppings

Directions

1. Melt coconut oil in pan over medium heat.
2. Dice apple into medium size pieces.
3. Place in pan and sauté for 2-3 minutes, until golden brown on bottom.
4. Flip over and sprinkle with cinnamon. Sauté for an additional 2 minutes or until golden.
5. Serve immediately with a drizzle of almond butter and unsweetened coconut flakes.

Carrot Halwa

Bev Alam

Makes 4 servings

Ingredients N

- 3 carrots
- ½ cup coconut cream (place can in fridge overnight)
- 1 Tbsp butter or ghee
- 4 cardamom pods
- **Nuts to decorate (optional)**

Directions

1. Wash, peel and grate carrots (a food processor is helpful).
2. Melt the butter or ghee over medium heat in a wide skillet.
3. Add carrots and cook.
4. Reduced heat and simmer until soft, about 30 minutes.
5. Add coconut cream and continue simmering on low for another 10 minutes.
6. Remove from heat.
7. Crush the cardamom pods, remove green husks and crush the black seeds.
8. Sprinkle crushed cardamom and nuts on carrot and cream mixture.
9. Eat warm or cold.

This doesn't get very soft like traditional halwa as no sugar is used. It is tasty none the less!

~ Bev

Coconut Snowballs

Heather Page

Makes 15-20 bites

Ingredients N

- ¾ cup crispy almonds (soaked and dried in a dehydrator, if possible)
- ¾ cup coconut butter
- 2 Tbsp coconut oil, melted
- ½ tsp vanilla
- ⅛ tsp cinnamon
- ⅛ tsp salt
- 2 Tbsp raw cacao nibs
- ½ cup organic dried coconut flakes

Directions

1. Process coconut flakes in food processor until coarsely chopped (about 5-10 seconds). Set aside in a small bowl.
2. Place almonds in food processor and pulse until coarsely chopped, with no large pieces (about 20-40 pulses).
3. Add coconut butter, coconut oil, vanilla, cinnamon and salt and mix until incorporated.
4. Add cacao nibs and pulse about 5-10 times to mix in.
5. Roll mixture into 1 inch balls and then roll in coconut flakes. Can be served immediately or chilled in refrigerator in an air tight container.

Chocolate Macadamia Coconut Clusters

Heather Page

Makes 10 clusters

Ingredients N

- **⅓ cup dry roasted salted macadamia nuts, chopped**
- ⅓ cup coconut flakes, roughly chopped
- ½ tsp vanilla
- ¼ cup coconut butter
- 2 Tbsp coconut oil
- 1 Tbsp raw cacao powder
- Pinch of himalayan sea salt

Directions

1. Melt coconut oil and butter on low, then add remaining ingredients except for the salt, and mix.
2. Spoon mixture into mini muffin cups.
3. Sprinkle with himalayan sea salt.
4. Place in freezer until hardened, about 15-20 minutes.

Chocolate Covered Banana Sandwich

Tiana Rockwell

Makes 18-20 sandwiches

Ingredients F, N

- **3 green tipped bananas**
- **½ cup raw almond butter**
- 4 oz 100% dark chocolate or 6-8 Tbsp raw cacao
- ½ cup unsweetened shredded coconut (optional)
- **½ cup raw nuts, chopped (optional)**

Directions

1. Line a baking sheet with a piece of wax paper.
2. Peel bananas. Slice on a slight angle into coins that are approximately ½ inch thick.
3. Spread a small amount of almond butter between two banana coins to make a sandwich.
4. Place banana sandwiches onto the prepared baking sheet and place in the freezer for approximately 1 hour.
5. Just before removing the frozen banana sandwiches, melt the 100% dark chocolate in a double broiler on the stove. Heat slowly as to not burn the chocolate. If using raw cacao add to sauce pan with ¼ cup filtered water and stir continuously on low flame till mixed.
6. Remove the bananas from the freezer and dip each sandwich into the melted chocolate/ raw cacao mixture. If desired, immediately dip into a bowl of unsweetened shredded coconut or chopped raw nuts and place back onto the wax paper.
7. Place the chocolate covered banana sandwiches into the freezer for an additional hour.
8. Remove the banana sandwiches and let them sit at room temperature for approximately 5 minutes before consuming. Then, ENJOY!

Coconut Bombs

Courtney Canfield Cronk

Makes 12-16 bites

Ingredients

- 16 oz package of unsweetened shredded coconut
- ½ cup coconut oil
- 2 tsp vanilla extract
- **Almonds or other nuts (optional)**
- Cinnamon (optional)

Directions

1. Blend shredded coconut in a food processor or high power blender.
2. Drizzle in coconut oil while blending until mixture is smooth like warm butter.
3. Pour mixture into a glass measuring cup.
4. Prep mini muffin tin with liners.
5. Place almonds or other nuts in bottom of each cup (1-3 almonds in each).
6. Fill each cup with mixture, being careful not to over fill.
7. Sprinkle cinnamon on top.
8. Place in fridge or freezer until hardened.
9. Store in fridge between eating.

Variations

Try adding zest of one lemon and top with a blueberry.
Add a few raw cacao nibs in each cup with almond.

Chocolate Chia Pudding
Kariman Pierce

Makes 4 servings

Ingredients N, F

- **¼ cup chia seeds**
- 1 cup **almond** or coconut milk
- 1 Tbsp raw cacao powder
- **½-1 green tipped banana (to taste)**

Directions

1. Add milk, chia seeds, banana and raw cacao powder (in that order) to blender.
2. Turn on blender to lowest setting and slowly increase speed to high. Blend until mixture turns thick (approximately 1 minute).
3. Eat immediately or put in fridge to chill and thicken more.

It is a good idea to go slow on the blender at first. This step is important to successfully keep the chia seeds from splashing up the side of the blender.

~ Kariman

Chocolate Avocado Pudding

Jeni Hall

Makes 2 servings

Ingredients F, NS

- **1 green-tipped banana**
- 1 avocado (mushy to the touch)
- ¼ cup cocoa powder/raw cacao powder
- ¼ cup coconut milk or **nut** milk (optional)

Directions

1. Blend all ingredients in a food processor/blender until smooth.
2. If you want it thicker, leave out the milk. If you want it a bit creamier and thinner, add the milk.

Chill for a few hours/overnight for best results!

~ Jeni

Beverages

Homemade Almond Milk

Tiana Rockwell

Makes 4 servings

Ingredients N

- **1 cup organic, raw almonds**
- 4 cups filtered water
- 1 vanilla bean (optional) OR 1 tsp vanilla extract

Directions

1. Place almonds in a mason jar and fill with water. Cover with a dish towel and soak almonds overnight for 8-12 hours.
2. Strain almonds in a metal colander and rinse thoroughly.
3. Place 4 cups filtered water, soaked almonds and whole vanilla bean or vanilla extract in a blender and blend for 60 seconds.
4. Pour nut milk mixture through a fine mesh metal strainer or a nut milk bag. Press pulp to release as much liquid as possible.
5. Discard any pulp left (or save for other uses).
6. If strainer was used, place a piece of cheesecloth in the strainer and pour the nut milk back through the strainer. Using both hands, pick up the sides of the cheesecloth and ring out the nut mixture. Discard the cheesecloth (or shake out the almond pulp and save for other uses).
7. Pour the nut milk into a mason jar, cover and refrigerate. The nut milk will last in the refrigerator for 3-4 days.

This milk can be made with any of your favorite raw, organic nuts.
Soak times are as follows:
Almonds 8-12 hours
Cashews: 2 hours
Pecans: 4-6 hours
Walnuts: 4 hours

~ Tiana

Basic Cashew Cream/Milk

Kariman Pierce

Makes 4 servings

Ingredients N

- **1 cup raw cashews**
- 2 cups filtered water for soaking
- ¼ cup to ¾ cup filter water for blending

Optional

- ½ tsp vanilla extract
- pinch of sea salt

Directions

1. Place raw cashews in a bowl with water, cover with a dish towel and soak for 2 - 4 hours.
2. Drain water and place cashews in a blender.
3. Add ¼ cup of water, optional ingredients and blend.
4. Add another ¼ - ½ cup water until desired thickness is reached.

Make Cashew Cream thick and eat with berries and nuts. Make it thinner and use for soups such as Kristi's Cream of Celery Soup (p. 74)

~ Kariman

Grapefruit Granita

Bev Alam

Makes 4 servings

Ingredients F

- **1 grapefruit**
- ¾ cup water

Directions

1. Segment the grapefruit.
2. Place water and grapefruit segments in a blender.
3. Pulse a few times to break up segments.
4. Pour into shallow glass dish.
5. Freeze for about 4 hours or until frozen.
6. Place chunks of ice in blender and pulse until desired consistency reached (alternatively use a fork to shave the ice).

This is refreshing on a warm day.

~ Bev

Simple Smoothie

Kariman Pierce

Makes 2 servings

Ingredients F, N

- 1 cup of coconut or **almond milk**
- **½ green-tipped banana (could be frozen)**
- **¼ cup blueberries (could be frozen)**
- 1 generous handful of greens
- 1 cup of clean ice
- 1 serving of single ingredient protein powder (**hemp**, pea or gelatin)

Directions

1. Place all ingredients in blender and pulse first, then blend till smooth.
2. Enjoy!

Favorite Blended Green Juice

Tara Chatterton

Ingredients F

- 1-2 cups coconut water
- 1-2 cups filtered or spring water
- 1 small Persian cucumber
- 2 celery stalks
- ½" - 1" knob of ginger
- **1 green apple**
- Small bunch of mint leaves
- Handful of spinach leaves
- Squeeze of lemon

Directions

1. Blend together in a blender and pour into a large bottle or tall glass.
2. Drink fresh with the pulp and shake or add more water as needed.

Breakfast Egg Shake

Makes 1 serving

Ingredients F, N

- 4-6 ounces non-dairy milk of your choice (coconut or **almond**)
- 1-2 raw pastured eggs
- **¼ cup blueberries**
- **½ green tipped banana**
- (optional) ¼ cup plain coconut or **almond** yogurt
- (optional) ¼ teaspoon vanilla extract
- (optional) pinch of nutmeg
- (optional) pinch of cinnamon

Directions

1. Blend all for 3 seconds – just enough to blend the eggs.
2. Pour and serve.

This smoothie can be made with a variety of ingredients. Other options include: drizzle in coconut oil while blending, replace eggs with 100% hemp, collagen/gelatin or pea protein.

Fermented Foods & Beverages

Why should you eat fermented foods?

Tricia Class

Fermented foods add beneficial bacteria to the intestine. They aid digestion by kick starting the process and contributing additional enzymes which help to break down fats in the liver. In addition, fermented foods heal the gut lining. This allows your body to actually utilize the nutrients from other foods. Pretty powerful stuff, huh? And fermented foods really taste good!

A word of caution on ferments: If you are not used to fermented foods then start off slowly. Drink no more than a quarter cup or eat 2 Tbsp of a fermented food if you are not accustomed to doing so. Then, slowly increase your consumption every few days. Drinking or eating a lot of fermented foods, if your body is not used to it, can lead to gastrointestinal upset. Why? These live active cultures, from fermented foods are powerful healers of your digestive track. They are also new to the environment. The current resident "culture" of your gut may not be used to the new neighbors yet.

Sauerkraut is the most basic and traditional fermented food. You can read further about its benefits and the benefits of other fermented foods in such great resources as "The Art of Fermentation" by Sandor Katz and "Nourishing Traditions" by Sally Fallon.

Sauerkraut

Makes 1-2 quarts

Ingredients

- 1 head of Cabbage
- 1-2 Tbsp of salt
- 1 clove of garlic, crushed
- Filtered water

Directions

1. Chop the cabbage into strips or squares.
2. Place cabbage in large bowl. With a mallet or some type of pounder, begin to gently pound the cabbage to release its juices. Keep pounding until the juices in the bowl cover the cabbage in the bowl.
3. Then transfer the contents of the bowl to a large glass jar (or two).
4. Add the garlic, salt and enough water to cover the cabbage to about an inch above the mixture.
5. Close the jar (but not too tightly) and set on counter at room temperature for 3-5 days.
6. "Burp" jar once a day to release build up of pressure.
7. Once fermented to your taste, place in the fridge and enjoy.

If adding other vegetables to your ferment, add them AFTER pounding the cabbage. No need to pound other vegetables.

Vegetable Combination Suggestions

- Cabbage and Carrots
- Carrots and Cauliflower
- Apples, Carrots, Cauliflower
- Apple, Cabbage, Cauliflower

Fennel, Carrot & Beet Kraut

Heather Page

Makes 1 quart

Ingredients

- ½ large cabbage, outer leaves removed and cleaned
- 2 beets, peeled and cleaned
- 1 fennel bulb, outer part removed and cleaned
- 2 large carrots peeled and cleaned
- 1 ½ - 2 Tbsp unrefined sea salt (pink or Real Brand salt)

Directions

1. Shred all ingredients in food processor.
2. Transfer to a clean bowl and sprinkle salt over contents. With clean and dry hands, mix all ingredients together to incorporate salt. Using a potato masher or pounding tool, mash kraut until liquid appears (vegetables will reduce to about half in bowl).
3. Pour into a sterilized and cooled quart jar and press kraut down until submerged under the brine/juice. Leave about an inch or two at the top of jar for space.
4. Close the jar (but not too tightly) and set on counter at room temperature for 3-5 days.
5. "Burp" jar once a day to release build up of pressure and to make sure kraut is submerged under brine to prevent mold.
6. Place in refrigerator to slow fermentation. Store in fridge.

Grapefruit-Ginger Carrot Kvass

Annette Steward

Makes 2 quarts

Ingredients

- 6 carrots, sliced into approx. ⅛ inch rounds
- 2 Tbsp roughly chopped ginger
- 6 large strips of organic grapefruit peel
- 4 tsp sea salt
- Filtered water
- One 2 quart jar with 2 piece lid

Directions

1. Wash, peel and chop carrots, and ginger. Ginger is easily peeled with a spoon, taking off only the skin.

2. Wash the grapefruit and use a vegetable peeler to get 6 large strips of peel, being careful not to go to deep as the pith can be bitter.

3. Put carrots, ginger, and grapefruit peel into a 2 quart jar. Add salt and fill the remainder of the jar with water, leaving 1 inch of space at the top.

4. Cover tightly with a lid and band. Gently shake well to dissolve the salt. Now do a test, push down and let up a few times and listen for a clicking noise. Perfect!

5. Let your kvass sit out on your kitchen counter or in a warm room preferably 68-72 degrees and out of direct sunlight for 3 days. You will know your kvass is done when you push down and release the lid and it doesn't make the clicking noise any longer. Depending on the temperature in your home your fermenting time may vary.

6. Once it's done move it to the refrigerator.

Drink up to 4 ounces of kvass morning and evening. When your kvass is down to about a ¼ of a jar, refill with filtered water leaving an inch of space at the top. Put your lid and band on nice and tight and leave it out on the counter again, and in 3 days you will have your second batch. This one will not be as strong as the first batch. Once you consume all of your kvass from the second ferment, throw away the ingredients and start over.

~ Annette

Granny Smith Apples &
Golden Beet Fermented Tonic

Hollis Baley

Makes 2 quarts

Ingredients F

- **1 Granny Smith apple cut into small square pieces**
- 1 golden beet cut into small square pieces
- 4 tsp sea salt or kosher salt
- Filtered water

Directions

1. Add apples, beets and sea salt to a ½ gallon jar.
2. Fill with filtered water leaving 1 inch of room at the top, cap with an airtight lid and gently shake until salt is dissolved.
3. Let ferment at room temperature for 2-3 days.
4. Open and taste to make sure desired sourness is achieved. If so, place the jar in the fridge and drink daily as a healthy fermented tonic.

You can re-use the vegetables for one more fermentation round when the liquid is just above the apples and beets in the jar. Simply add 4 more tsp sea salt, fill with filtered water and repeat fermentation process as outlined above.

~ Hollis

Resources

Helpful Kitchen Tools

- Wooden cutting boards (use separate ones for meats vs. vegetables/fruits)
- Kitchen knives
- Mixing bowls
- Measuring spoons
- Measuring cups for liquids
- Measuring cups for dry ingredients
- Wooden spoons
- Spatula
- Ladle
- Tongs
- Colander/strainer
- Frying pan
- Saute pan
- Sauce pan
- Stock pot
- Dutch oven
- Roasting pan
- Baking dishes
- Cookie sheet
- Muffin tin
- Blender
- Immersion or hand blender
- Food processor
- Crock pot or slow cooker
- Pressure cooker
- Glass food storage containers
- Parchment paper

A Note About Cookware:

In the RESTART® Program, we care about the quality of the ingredients in your meals, and we also care about the quality of the tools you cook with. We recommend cooking with pots, pans, tools and utensils made from safe, non-toxic materials to avoid adding any unwanted chemicals to your meal. Aluminum, plastics and Teflon are some of the worst offenders when it comes to transferring harmful chemicals to your food, so work to transition away from these materials. Instead choose stainless steel, glass, or cast iron for cooking. If you don't want to give up non-stick surfaces, try quality enameled or ceramic coated pans instead of Teflon. Use wooden cutting boards instead of plastic. A little baking soda and lemon will keep your wooden boards clean and sanitary. Store your food in glass instead of plastic. Protect your food from touching aluminum surfaces like cookie sheets or foil by using parchment paper. These are just a few ways to keep your food as healthy as you intended!

What's in your Pantry?

- Apple Cider Vinegar
- Raw, Virgin Coconut Oil
- Unsweetened Shredded Coconut Flakes
- Coconut Butter
- Cans of full-fat Coconut Milk
- Coconut Wraps
- Coconut Flour
- Almond Flour (or Meal)
- Almond Butter
- Cashew Butter
- Any Nut Butter
- Tahini
- Any raw, dry roasted or sprouted nuts
- Sesame Seeds
- Pumpkin Seeds
- Hemp Seeds
- Flax Seeds
- Chia Seeds
- Pink Himalayan Sea Salt
- Other varieties of Sea Salt
- Sardines in water or olive oil
- Smoked Oysters in water or olive oil

- Cans of Wild-caught Tuna or Salmon
- Fish Sauce
- Coconut Aminos
- Gluten-Free Tamari Soy Sauce
- Avocado Oil
- Ghee
- Extra Virgin Olive Oil
- Cold Pressed Sesame Oil
- Cold Pressed Infused Olive Oil
- Herbal Teas such as roasted dandelion root, red raspberry leaf, rooibos
- Black, Green & White Teas
- Coffee Beans
- Cinnamon
- Ginger
- Pumpkin Pie Spice
- Vanilla, Almond, and/or Peppermint Extract
- Grass-fed Gelatin/Collagen Peptides
- Raw Cacao Powder
- Cans of Diced Tomatoes

This Cooking Techniques section is designed to describe several different cooking methods. Experiment with different ways to prepare your foods and discover how easy and enjoyable it can be!

Basic Cooking Techniques

Sauté

Best Food Choices

Tender meats, fish, poultry, veggies. Seasonings can include: marinades, dry spice rubs, or a simple sprinkling of sea salt and pepper.

What It Is

Preparing foods quickly using any kind of fat in a pan over medium to high heat. The coating of fat helps with heat transfer and protects the food from burning. Sautéing holds the nutritional value of foods because the foods are fresh and the cooking time is a quick.

How To

Using sauté pan and medium to medium high heat, add fat while pan is heating. Stir food with wooden spoon until desired doneness. Serve sautéd foods right away.

Note

Tender veggies like spinach and mushrooms can go directly into the sauté pan. Denser items like root veggies should be par cooked before sautéing. Meats, poultry, fish, etc. should be sliced, pounded, etc. in order to make them thinner.

Stir Fry

Best Food Choices

Tender meats, fish, poultry, veggies

What It Is

Similar to sautéing. The difference is that the food is cut into smaller pieces/strip and kept constantly moving during the cooking process. Woks are traditionally used because of their shape but a large pan works well, too. Foods requiring longest cooking time should be added first.

How To

Heat pan first, then add fat. Using a wok or large pan, placed on high heat, add foods, stir constantly until done!

Broiling

Best food choices

ANY

What It Is

The heat source comes from the top of the oven, with the food placed close to heat source (but not touching it). Typically a fast process as the heat is so high. Meats and fish retain their moisture and flavor perfectly when the skin is left on.

How To

Place food on broiling pan (that comes with the oven) Preheat broiler until hot then place food under the heat on top rack and stay nearby! Check after every minute or two until done. This is fast!

Roasting & Baking

Best Food Choices

Larger foods; whole or parts of poultry, larger cuts of meat, denser (root) veggies

What It Is

Hot air cooks the food, additional fat is not required for meats. Larger pieces are used (fish, poultry, meats, etc.) When roasting veggies, cover in fats and seasonings before roasting, exception: sea salt, add that after roasting.

How To

Preheat oven, place food in roasting pan with desired seasonings, place in middle rack until done. Check with meat thermometer for desired doneness.

Steaming

Best Food Choices

All veggies

What It Is

To quickly and lightly cook foods without fats (add those later!)

How To

Fill a pot with an inch or two of water. Place veggies to be steamed in a steaming basket over the water (but not touching it). Cover and let steam for about 5 minutes or until desired tenderness. Drain, reserve the water to use in soups, etc.

Stewing & Braising

Best Food Choices

Denser meats and root veggies

What It Is

Cooking in a flavorful liquid. The liquid becomes the sauce.

How To

Cooking time is longer and at lower heat to cook more gently. Put food in deep heavy pot. Sear meats (quickly cook outside of meat in fats to develop flavor and color), then cover with liquid (broth, water with aromatic herbs added, etc.) Gently simmer, covering in the beginning. Toward the end of cooking time remove covering so that the liquid reduces to a sauce consistency. Typically takes 2-4 hours depending on the weight and size of food (e.g. a 1 pound pot roast takes about 3 hrs).

Note

Best prepared a day in advance to allow the flavors to mature fully.

 Many of these ideas need some "prep ahead" time. Collect small containers or bags and fill them ahead of time with several portions for yourself. Place them in your pantry or fridge and they will be ready to "grab and go"!

Grab and Go Snacks

- Avocado & Sauerkraut (p. 125)
- Avocado & Bacon wrapped in a lettuce leaf
- Baked Kale Chips
- Toasted Coconut Flakes with Cinnamon and Himalayan Sea Salt (p. 108)
- Celery with Almond Butter
- (Sugar-free) Beef Jerky (p. 25)
- Hard-boiled Egg
- Left-over Chicken and Cucumber slices
- Pickles, traditionally fermented
- Any nuts! Macadamia, Pistachio, Pecan, Cashew, Walnut
- Cold cuts rolled with Avocado, Carrots & Mustard
- Deviled Eggs
- Lettuce wrap with leftovers
- Smoked Salmon wrapped Cucumber spears
- Chopped Raw Veggies - Jicama, Carrots, Cucumber, Celery, Broccoli with Creamy Coconut-Basil Pesto (p. 94), Ranch Dressing (p. 84) or Guacamole (p. 89)
- Tuna or Egg Salad with Basic Mayonnaise (p. 91)
- Green Apple with Coconut Butter
- Muffins (pgs. 102-105)
- Berries in Coconut Milk
- Basic Meatballs (p. 28) or Ann's Turkey Meatballs (p. 34) with Mustard or Creamy Coconut-Basil Pesto (p. 94)
- Chocolate Chia Pudding (p. 115)
- Chocolate Avocado Pudding (p. 116)
- Favorite Blended Green Juice (p. 121)
- Simple Smoothie (p. 121)
- Mug of Bone Broth (pgs. 81-82)

RESTART® One Week Meal Plan

Your life is busy! We can all relate to that. One of the reasons many people express frustration when trying to adopt healthier eating habits is that they approach mealtime and don't know what to make. Or maybe they don't have the ingredients they need to pull together a healthy meal, so they choose less-healthy convenience foods instead. Sound familiar?

Eating fresh, whole foods means you must get in the kitchen. Setting aside extra preparation time once or twice a week can ensure that you always have great choices available. The time you spend will pay off in healthy dividends for you and your family.

This meal plan is just one example of what a week of healthy choices could look like. The plan includes recipes from this cookbook, plus instructions for pre-preparation that will make life simpler later in the week. Notice that many of the meals provide for convenient leftovers!

You will also find a shopping list that corresponds with the ingredients you will need to make all the meals included. Set aside time to shop twice a week for the freshest ingredients. The recipes are designed for two people. If you have a larger family, adjust accordingly.

The plan includes a variety of proteins, fats and non-starchy vegetables. It also includes a variety of textures, colors and tastes because food should be enjoyed with all of our senses! You can use this plan exactly as it is, or as a template to get you started on your own meal planning. The goal is for you to develop a pattern of preparation with the healthy choices you enjoy the most. Happy Planning!

Sunday:
Shopping Day

AM: Shop for "Sunday Grocery List", cook 1 pkg bacon/sausage, bake Almond Spice Muffins (p. 105), hard boil 12 eggs, chop preferred vegetables for Tuesday snack, grill tuna for Monday lunch (optional)

Breakfast: Veggie Frittata (p. 12)

Lunch: Ann's Turkey Meatballs (p. 34) with Oven Roasted Vegetables (p. 66)

Dinner: Roast Chicken (p. 41) with Brussels Sprouts with Bacon (p. 60) (Save 2 cups chicken for Monday dinner)

Snack: Almond Spice Muffins

PM: Put chicken carcass and add vegetables scraps (optional) in slow cooker and make Chicken Bone Broth (p. 82) over night

Monday:

AM: Strain and refrigerate Chicken Broth

Breakfast: Almond Spice Muffins and Bacon

Lunch: Niçoise Salad (p. 52)

Dinner: Indian Chicken Curry with Cauliflower and Asparagus (p. 38) with Creamy Coconut Kale (p. 72)

Snack: Green Apple & Almond butter

PM: Make Kristi's Cream of Celery Soup (p. 74) and prep vegetables for Create-a-Salad (p. 71) for Tuesday lunch

Tuesday:

AM: Assemble salad for lunch

Breakfast: Leftover Veggie Frittata

Lunch: Kristi's Cream of Celery Soup & Create-a-Salad

Dinner: Leftover Turkey Meatballs with Creamy Zucchini Noodles (p. 69)

Snack: Hard-boiled Egg with Vegetables

PM: Make Coconut Bombs (p. 114)

Wednesday:
Shopping Day

AM:	Shop for "Wednesday Grocery List", thaw ground beef for dinner
Breakfast:	Baked Avocado with Egg (p. 13) with Bacon or Sausage
Lunch:	Leftover Indian Chicken Curry with Cauliflower and Asparagus with Creamy Coconut Kale
Dinner:	Ground Beef with Cabbage and Kale (p. 24)
Snack:	Berries with Coconut Bombs
PM:	Make Egg Muffins (p. 16) & Chocolate Avocado Pudding (p. 116)

Thursday:

Breakfast:	Egg Muffins
Lunch:	Leftover Ground Beef with Cabbage and Kale
Dinner:	Simple Salmon with Asparagus (p. 50) and Mashed Cauliflower (p. 63)
Snack:	Chocolate Avocado Pudding
PM:	Take chicken wings out of freezer and thaw in refrigerator, chop preferred vegetables for Friday dinner

Friday:

Breakfast:	Leftover Egg Muffins
Lunch:	Leftover Simple Salmon with Asparagus
Dinner:	Chicken Wings (p. 42) with vegetables and Ranch Dressing (p. 84)
Snack:	Leftover Berries with Coconut Bombs
PM:	Cook a second package of bacon for pancakes (if needed) while you cook the chicken and set it aside for the morning

Saturday:

Breakfast:	Bacon Pancakes (p. 98) with Sautéed Green Apple with Cinnamon (p. 109)
Lunch:	Leftover Chicken Wings and vegetables with Ranch Dressing
Dinner:	Scallops with Shiitake Mushrooms in Ginger Sauce (p. 49) and Aunt Karin's Ginger Carrots (p. 72)
Snack:	Toasted Coconut Flakes with Cinnamon and Himalayan Sea Salt (p. 108) and 1 ounce of nuts

Sunday Shopping List

- ☐ 3 Green Apples
- ☐ 1 pkg Blueberries
- ☐ 2 green-tipped Bananas
- ☐ 4 large Yellow Onions
- ☐ 2 Red Onions
- ☐ 1 Cucumber
- ☐ 1 bunch Radishes
- ☐ 1 head Cauliflower
- ☐ 1 lb. Asparagus
- ☐ 3 medium Zucchini
- ☐ 2 Avocados
- ☐ 2 bunches Celery
- ☐ Scallions
- ☐ 2 ea. Red, Yellow, Orange Bell Peppers
- ☐ 1 lb. Lemons
- ☐ 2 lb. Brussels Sprouts
- ☐ 2 Leeks
- ☐ 2 medium Parsnips
- ☐ 1 pkg Carrots
- ☐ 1 large Turnip or Beet
- ☐ 2-3 heads Garlic
- ☐ 1 medium Shallot
- ☐ 1 lg. piece fresh Ginger
- ☐ 1 10 oz. pkgs Kale
- ☐ 3 heads Boston or Leaf Lettuce
- ☐ 1 pkg Cherry & 1 lb Roma Tomatoes
- ☐ 1/2 lb. fresh Green Beans
- ☐ Butter or Ghee
- ☐ 3 dozen Pastured Eggs
- ☐ 2 pkg nitrate free Bacon
- ☐ 1 pkg nitrate free Breakfast Sausage
- ☐ 1 lb Ground Turkey

- ☐ 4-5 lb. whole Organic Chicken
- ☐ 1 lb. Tuna Steaks or 2 cans Tuna
- ☐ 1 can Tomato Paste
- ☐ 1 28 6rfoz. can Crushed Tomatoes
- ☐ 1 can Green Chilies
- ☐ Creamy Almond Butter
- ☐ Almond Meal
- ☐ Baking Soda
- ☐ Baking Cups
- ☐ Raw Apple Cider Vinegar
- ☐ 2 cans full fat Coconut Milk
- ☐ 1 jar Capers (optional)
- ☐ 1 jar Anchovies (optional)
- ☐ Dijon Mustard
- ☐ 1 lb. Cashews
- ☐ Almonds or other nuts (optional)
- ☐ Tahini (sesame paste)
- ☐ Nutritional Yeast
- ☐ 1 pkg unsweetened Shredded Coconut
- ☐ Gluten Free Vanilla Extract
- ☐ Olive Oil
- ☐ Coconut Oil
- ☐ Rosemary, fresh and dried
- ☐ Thyme, fresh and dried
- ☐ Parsley, fresh   ☐ Cilantro, fresh
- ☐ Oregano, fresh and dried
- ☐ Basil, fresh   ☐ Marjoram, dried
- ☐ Bay Leaf, dried   ☐ Turmeric
- ☐ Cumin   ☐ Pumpkin Pie Spice
- ☐ Cinnamon   ☐ Ground Nutmeg
- ☐ Ground Ginger   ☐ Smoked Paprika
- ☐ Sea salt   ☐ Black Pepper

RESTART

140

Wednesday Shopping List

- ❏ 3 green-tipped Bananas
- ❏ 3 Green Apples
- ❏ 3-4 Lemons
- ❏ 1 head Cabbage
- ❏ 1 head Cauliflower
- ❏ 1 bunch Kale
- ❏ 1 lb. Carrots
- ❏ I bunch Celery
- ❏ 1 Cucumber
- ❏ Green or Red Pepper
- ❏ Scallions
- ❏ 2 Avocados, ripe
- ❏ 1 lb. Asparagus
- ❏ 1 head Garlic
- ❏ 2 Yellow Onions
- ❏ 1 lb. Shiitake Mushrooms
- ❏ Snow Peas
- ❏ Chives, fresh and dried
- ❏ Dill, fresh
- ❏ Parsley, fresh
- ❏ 1 dozen Pastured Eggs
- ❏ 1 lb. Organic Ground Beef, grass fed
- ❏ 2 lbs. Organic Chicken Wings
- ❏ 1 lb. Wild Alaskan Salmon fillets
- ❏ 1 lb large Sea Scallops
- ❏ 1 pkg nitrate-free Bacon
- ❏ Almond Milk (carrageenan free)
- ❏ Cocoa Powder or Raw Cacao Powder

- ❏ Yellow Mustard
- ❏ Walnut or Avocado oil
- ❏ Coconut Flour
- ❏ Purified Granular Gelatin
- ❏ 1 pkg. unsweetened Coconut Flakes
- ❏ 1 can full fat Coconut Milk

OTHER:

_____
_____
_____
_____
_____
_____
_____
_____
_____
_____

NOTES

NOTES

Made in the USA
Middletown, DE
27 March 2018